AMERICAN POLITICAL, ECONOMIC, AND SECURITY ISSUES SERIES

FEDERAL SPENDING: A RIDDLE WRAPPED UP IN AN ENIGMA

American Political, Economic, and Security Issues Series

The Land and Maritime Boundary Disputes of the Americas
Rongxing Guo (Editor)
2009. ISBN: 978-1-60741-636-4

Foreign Investment In U.S. Securities
Declan J. Byrne (Editor)
2010. ISBN: 978-1-60876-084-8

Federal Spending: A Riddle Wrapped up in an Enigma
Frederick C. Hargis
2010. ISBN: 978-1-60741-728-6

AMERICAN POLITICAL, ECONOMIC, AND SECURITY ISSUES SERIES

FEDERAL SPENDING: A RIDDLE WRAPPED UP IN AN ENIGMA

FREDERICK C. HARGIS
EDITOR

Nova Science Publishers, Inc.

New York

For permission to use material from this book please contact us:
Telephone 631-231-7269; Fax 631-231-8175
Web Site: http://www.novapublishers.com

LIBRARY OF CONGRESS CATALOGING-IN-PUBLICATION DATA

Federal spending : a riddle wrapped up in an enigma / editors, Frederick C. Hargis.
p. cm.
Includes index.
ISBN 978-1-60741-728-6 (hardcover)
1. Government spending policy--United States. 2. United States--Appropriations and expenditures. 3. Debts, Public--United States. I. Hargis, Frederick C.
HJ7537.F43 2009
336.3'90973--dc22
2009031740

Published by Nova Science Publishers, Inc. † New York

CONTENTS

PREFACE

This book looks at the three broad categories of federal spending; discretionary spending, mandatory spending, and net interest. Mandatory spending includes federal government spending on entitlement programs and Food Stamps as well as other budget outlays controlled by laws other than appropriation acts. Entitlement programs such as Social Security and Medicare make up the bulk of mandatory spending. Discretionary spending is provided and controlled through appropriations acts. Mandatory spending accounts for over half of total federal spending and almost a ninth of gross domestic product (GDP). Those three programs, therefore, make up over 40% of federal spending. In the long term, projections suggest that if current policies remain unchanged, the U.S. faces a major fiscal imbalance, largely due to rising health care costs and impending Baby Boomer retirements.

Chapter 1 - Of the three broad categories of federal spending, the only category that cannot be reduced by legislative action is net interest payments. Net interest payments accounted for about 7% of federal spending between 1962 and the late 1970s. With the high interest rates in the late 1970s and the large budget deficits in the 1980s, net interest payments eventually rose to 15% of federal spending. The low interest rates combined with budget discipline in the 1990s reduced net interest payments back down to 7% of federal outlays by 2003. However, net interest payments have recently increased and are projected to continue increasing in the near-term.

Federal spending is divided into three broad categories. First, discretionary spending is provided and controlled by the annual appropriations acts and includes such things as defense and education spending.[1] Discretionary spending currently accounts for about 40% of federal outlays. Second, direct or mandatory spending is provided and controlled by laws other than appropriation acts and includes spending for such programs as Social Security and Medicare.[2] Mandatory spending accounts for over half of federal outlays. Lastly, net interest payments are interest payments on federal debt held by the public and currently account for almost 9% of federal outlays.

In an effort to reduce spending, the FY2006 budget resolution (H.Con.Res. 95) included reconciliation instructions to reduce mandatory spending by $35 billion over the next five years. Congress ultimately voted to reduce mandatory spending by about $40 billion over five years. In addition, Congress enacted a 1% across-the-board reduction in FY2006 discretionary spending. The only category of federal spending that cannot be reduced by legislative action (barring default on the public debt) is net interest payments.

While Congress cannot affect current net interest payments, congressional actions on the budget will affect future interest payments. This chapter examines net interest payments and the mechanisms through which Congress can affect net interest payments.

Chapter 2 - Chapter 2 - This chapter is edited and excerpted testimony by David M. Walker, Comptroller General of the United States, before the U.S. House of Representatives, Budget Committee on February 15, 2006.

Chapter 3 - This chapter reviews trends in mandatory spending since 1962 and discusses CBO baseline projections of mandatory spending, which extend to 2018. The report examines mandatory spending's growth relative to total federal spending and to the size of the U.S. economy, and looks at how the composition of mandatory spending has changed.

Chapter 4 - Prepared as part of GAO's basic statutory responsibility for monitoring the condition of the nation's finances, the objectives of this chapter were to (1) determine the feasibility of designing and using trigger mechanisms to constrain growth in mandatory spending programs and (2) provide an analysis of the factors that led to differences between estimated and actual outlays in seven mandatory budget accounts during fiscal years 2000 through 2004.

Chapter 5 - Discretionary spending is provided in, and controlled by, annual appropriations acts, which fund many of the routine activities commonly associated with such federal government functions as running executive branch agencies, congressional offices and agencies, and international operations of the government. Essentially all spending on federal wages and salaries is discretionary. Discretionary spending is often contrasted with mandatory, or direct, spending. Mandatory spending includes federal spending on entitlement programs, the Food Stamp program, and other spending controlled by laws other than appropriation acts. Spending levels for mandatory programs are generally controlled by eligibility criteria and size of the eligible population.

In: Federal Spending: A Riddle Wrapped ... ISBN: 978-1-60741-728-6
Editor: Frederick C. Hargis 2010 Nova Science Publishers, Inc.

Chapter 1

INTEREST PAYMENTS ON THE FEDERAL DEBT: A PRIMER

Thomas L. Hungerford

SUMMARY

Of the three broad categories of federal spending, the only category that cannot be reduced by legislative action is net interest payments. Net interest payments accounted for about 7% of federal spending between 1962 and the late 1970s. With the high interest rates in the late 1970s and the large budget deficits in the 1980s, net interest payments eventually rose to 15% of federal spending. The low interest rates combined with budget discipline in the 1990s reduced net interest payments back down to 7% of federal outlays by 2003. However, net interest payments have recently increased and are projected to continue increasing in the near-term.

Federal spending is divided into three broad categories. First, discretionary spending is provided and controlled by the annual appropriations acts and includes such things as defense and education spending.[1] Discretionary spending currently accounts for about 40% of federal outlays. Second, direct or mandatory spending is provided and controlled by laws other than appropriation acts and includes spending for such programs as Social Security and Medicare.[2] Mandatory spending accounts for over half of federal outlays. Lastly, net interest payments are interest payments on federal debt held by the public and currently account for almost 9% of federal outlays.

In an effort to reduce spending, the FY2006 budget resolution (H.Con.Res. 95) included reconciliation instructions to reduce mandatory spending by $35 billion over the next five years. Congress ultimately voted to reduce mandatory spending by about $40 billion over five years. In addition, Congress enacted a 1% across-the-board reduction in FY2006 discretionary spending. The only category of federal spending that cannot be reduced by legislative action (barring default on the public debt) is net interest payments.

While Congress cannot affect current net interest payments, congressional actions on the budget will affect future interest payments. This chapter examines net interest payments and the mechanisms through which Congress can affect net interest payments.

FEDERAL DEBT

Federal debt is composed of debt issued by the Treasury (Treasury securities) and debt securities issued by other federal agencies (agency securities). At the end of FY2008, total federal securities amounted to $10.0 trillion, of which only $23.1 billion (less than 0.3%) were agency securities. Federal debt is held either by the public (that is, private investors) or in government accounts. Currently, about 42% of federal debt is held in various government accounts. For example, the two Social Security trust funds currently hold about $2.4 trillion in Treasury securities. The rest of the federal debt is held by the public (foreign and domestic), including individuals, pension funds, banks, and other investors.

Figure 1 shows the level of total federal debt and debt held by the public since 1962 as a percentage of gross domestic product (GDP). Both measures of debt fell as a proportion of GDP between 1962 and the mid-1970s. Beginning in 1981, total federal debt began to climb as tax cuts, increases in defense spending, and a recession increased budget deficits. Total debt continued growing relative to GDP until the mid-1990s. As budget deficits gave way to budget surpluses after 1997, and as the economy expanded, federal debt fell as a percentage of GDP. The mild recession and the tax cuts in 2001 moved the federal budget back into deficit and federal debt consequently increased.

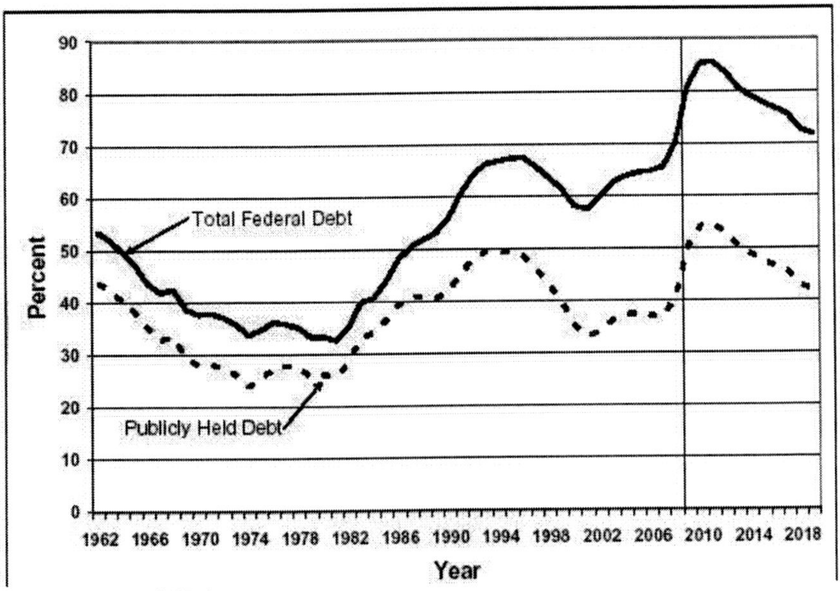

Source: OMB and CBO.

Figure 1. Total U.S. Federal Debt and Debt Held by the Public, FY1962-FY2019 (as a percentage of GDP)

Between 1962 and 1982, total federal debt and debt held by the public followed roughly parallel trends. After the mid-1980s, however, trends in total federal debt and debt held by the public began to diverge. This was mainly due to changes in the Social Security program enacted in 1983 which increased revenues and reduced the growth in benefit payments. As a result, the Social Security program began to run surpluses (surplus monies are invested in Treasury securities), increasing the share of federal debt held in government accounts. The Congressional Budget Office's (CBO) baseline projection indicates that total federal debt and debt held by the public will continue to diverge over the next 10 years.[3]

Interest Payments on the Federal Debt

In FY2008, total or gross interest on Treasury debt securities amounted to about $460 billion—about 15% of federal outlays. However, not all of this flowed from the Treasury to the public—about $210 billion was credited to government accounts such as the Social Security trust funds. The interest payments on the Treasury securities held in government accounts do not represent funds or real resources available for spending. Rather these interest payments are merely a bookkeeping entry transferring funds from one government account to another.[4]

The upper line in **Figure 2** shows the evolution of gross interest payments since 1962. Gross interest payments remained at about 7% to 8% of outlays until the late 1970s. After 1978, interest payments rapidly increased to reach almost 18% of outlays by 1997. After 1997, gross interest payments fell as a percentage of outlays as interest rates fell and the federal budget moved from deficit to surplus. When federal budget deficits reappeared in 2002, gross interest payments began rising.

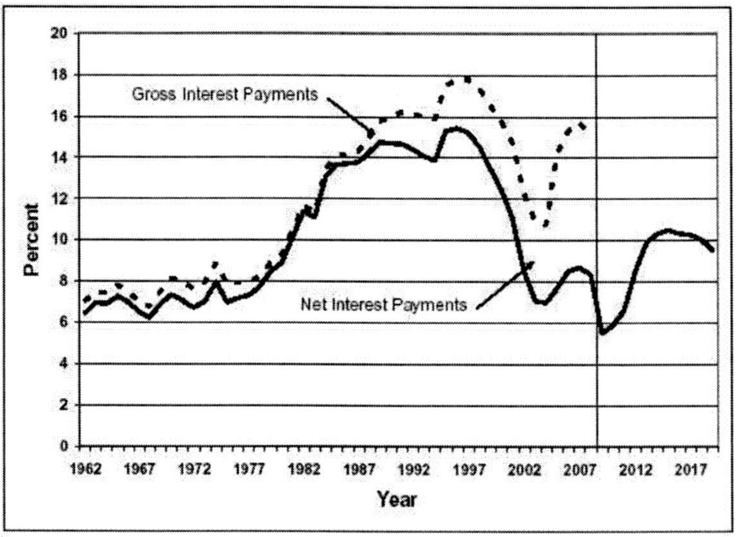

Source: OMB and CBO.

Figure 2. Gross and Net Interest on Treasury Debt Securities, FY1962-FY2019 (as a percentage of federal outlays)

Net interest payments are the component of gross interest payments that involves a transfer of funds or real resources from the government to the public. The lower line in **Figure 2** shows the evolution of net interest payments since 1962. For the most part, net interest payments followed the same basic trend as gross interest payments. However, the gap between gross and net interest payments widened after the mid-1980s.[5] As with gross interest payments, net interest payments fell as a percentage of federal outlays when federal debt declined in the late-1990s. Net interest payments began to increase in 2004 but leveled out because of falling interest rates. Additionally, net interest payments are projected to fall dramatically in 2009 due to very low interest rates. Large budget deficits in 2009 and 2010, however, will lead to rising net interest payments for the next five to six years.[6] CBO projects that, under plausible scenarios, net interest payments could continue rising indefinitely.[7]

DETERMINANTS OF NET INTEREST PAYMENTS

The primary determinants of net interest payments are (1) the interest rate or yield on U.S. Treasury securities, and (2) the level of debt held by the public. **Figure 3** shows the evolution of net interest payments, debt held by the public, and the interest rate since 1967. The interest rate is the yield on five-year constant maturity U.S. Treasury bonds. Both net interest payments and debt held by the public are expressed as a percentage of GDP, and are indexed so that the value in 1967 is equal to one.[8]

Net interest payments increased rapidly beginning in 1977 at about the same time that interest rates increased dramatically (see **Figure 3**). Net interest payments continued to increase after interest rates fell in the early 1980s because of the increase in debt held by the public. The increase in debt held by the public was due to the large budget deficits in the first years of the Reagan Administration and counteracted the effect of falling interest rates on net interest payments. As both interest rates and debt held by the public fell after 1997, net interest payments fell as a proportion of federal outlays.

The government can, to some extent, control the effective interest rate paid on its debt by varying the maturity of its securities. The federal government issues both short-term and long-term debt. The yield on Treasury securities varies with the maturity of the securities. Typically, short-term securities have a lower yield than longer-term securities, and the yield curve, therefore, is upward sloping.[9] Occasionally, the yield curve will invert with longer-term securities having a lower yield than short-term securities, but this happens neither often nor for extended periods.

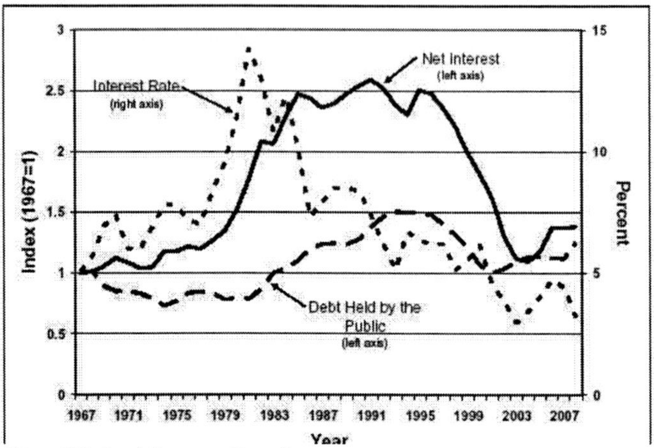

Source: OMB and Federal Reserve Board.

Figure 3. Interest Rate, Net Interest Payments, and Debt Held by the Public, FY1967-FY2008

A primary goal of debt management is to obtain the lowest borrowing cost over time.[10] Over the past 30 years, the mean maturity of marketable Treasury securities held by private investors has varied between about three years and six years. Since 2000, the range has narrowed to between five and six years. However, this apparent stability masks changes in the types of securities issued. In 2001, for example, the Treasury stopped issuing 30-year bonds.[11] Although shorter-term Treasury securities tend to have lower yields than longer-term securities, they also are more volatile. Consequently, the financing costs of short-term securities can change dramatically over fairly short periods. This volatility and uncertainty complicate efforts to obtain the lowest borrowing costs over time.

Congressional actions affecting the budget deficit will affect federal debt, which, in turn, affects future net interest payments. Budget deficits and federal debt can also affect the interest rates on Treasury securities.[12] Increasing federal debt will increase the supply of Treasury securities. This will tend to push down the price and increase the yield of these securities.[13] Recent studies have estimated that increasing debt held by the public by one percent of GDP will increase future interest rates by two to six basis points (0.02 to 0.06 percentage points).[14] Thus budget deficits increase federal debt and future interest rates, which in turn increase future net interest payments.

End Notes

[1] For more information on discretionary spending see CRS Report RL34424, *Trends in Discretionary Spending*, by D. Andrew Austin and Mindy R. Levit.

[2] For more information on mandatory spending see CRS Report RL33074, *Mandatory Spending Since 1962*, by D. Andrew Austin and Mindy R. Levit.

[3] CBO's baseline projection starts with Congress's most recent budgetary decisions and then assumes that no policy changes will be made over the projection period. For entitlement programs CBO assumes that current laws will continue unchanged and by law assumes that discretionary spending will grow at the rate of inflation throughout the projection period. For revenues, CBO assumes that the provisions in the 2001 and 2003 tax cuts will expire on schedule, and that more individuals will be subject to the alternative minimum tax (AMT). Furthermore, the baseline projection does not include the budgetary effects of any new stimulus legislation. CBO's baseline is not intended to be a prediction of future budgetary outcomes. See CBO, *The Long-term Budget Outlook*, December 2005 and CBO, *The Budget and Economic Outlook: Fiscal Years 2009 to 2019*, January 2009.

[4] In essence, the interest payments are used to purchase more Treasury securities. While not representing real resources available for current spending, the government will eventually have to find real resources (by raising taxes or reducing spending) for the redemption of these securities, under current law.

[5] The widening of this gap is due, in part, to the increases in the Social Security trust fund resulting from the 1983 amendments to the Social Security Act. These amendments led to increasing revenues to the Social Security program, and reduced the growth in benefits.

[6] CBO projects that the deficit will be almost $1,200 billion in 2009 and $703 billion in 2010. See CBO, *Budget and Economic Outlook*, January 2009.

[7] See CBO, *The Long-term Budget Outlook*, December 2005.

[8] The index is created by dividing the value in each year by the value in 1967. This is done so that both series fit on the same graph.

[9] The yield curve is the relationship of the yield on securities and the maturity of those securities.

[10] See CRS Report RL34682, *Federal Debt Management: Concepts, Options, and Policies* (1945-2008), by James M. Bickley.

[11] Treasury began issuing 30-year bonds again in February 2006.

[12] The strength of the economy, inflation expectations, and the actions of the Federal Reserve Board also have an important effect on interest rates.

[13] There is an inverse relationship between the price of a bond and the yield of the bond.

[14] See Eric Engen and R. Glenn Hubbard, *Federal Government Debts and Interest Rates*, National Bureau of Economic Research, Working Paper no. 10681, August 2004; William G. Gale and Peter R. Orszag, "Budget Deficits, National Saving, and Interest Rates," *Brookings Papers on Economic Activity*, vol. 2004, no. 2 (2004), pp. 101-187; and Thomas Laubach, *New Evidence on the Interest Rate Effects of Budget Deficits and Debt*, Board of Governors of the Federal Reserve System, Finance and Economics Discussion paper no. 2003-13, May 2003.

In: Federal Spending: A Riddle Wrapped ... ISBN: 978-1-60741-728-6
Editor: Frederick C. Hargis 2010 Nova Science Publishers, Inc.

Chapter 2

21ST CENTURY: ADDRESSING LONG-TERM FISCAL CHALLENGES MUST INCLUDE A RE-EXAMINATION OF MANDATORY SPENDING

United States Government Accountability Office

Mr. Chairman, Representative Spratt, and Members of the Committee:

I appreciate this opportunity to talk with you about the need to look at entitlement and other mandatory spending programs in light of our nation's long-term fiscal outlook and the challenge it poses for the budget and oversight processes.

As I have said many times before, meeting our nation's large, growing, and structural fiscal imbalance will require a three-pronged approach:

- restructuring existing entitlement programs,
- reexamining the base of discretionary and other spending, and
- reviewing and revising existing tax policy, including tax expenditures,[1] which can operate like mandatory spending programs.

Before I turn to the major driver of the long-term spending outlook— rising health care costs combined with known demographic trends—I'd like to step back and take a broader view of the need to reexamine and reconsider what the federal government does, how it does it, and who does it. We are in the first decade of the

21st century but the basis and design for many of the federal government's activities date from before I was born.

In our report entitled *21st Century Challenges: Reexamining the Base of the Federal Government,*[2] we presented illustrative questions for policy makers to consider as they carry out their responsibilities. These questions look across major areas of the budget and federal operations including discretionary and mandatory spending, and tax policies and programs. We hope that this chapter, among other things, will be used by various congressional committees as they consider which areas of government need particular attention and reconsideration. You will, of course, also receive more specific proposals, some of them will be presented within comprehensive agendas—the President's Budget released last week is just one very prominent example.

Our report provides examples of the kinds of difficult choices the nation faces with regard to discretionary spending; mandatory spending, including entitlements; as well as tax policies and compliance activities. It is, I think, important to recognize that tax policies and programs financing the federal budget can be reviewed not only with an eye toward the overall level of revenue provided to fund federal operations and commitments, but also the mix of taxes and the extent to which the tax code is used to promote overall economic growth and broad-based societal objectives. In practice, some tax expenditures are very similar to mandatory spending programs even though they are not subject to the appropriations process or selected budget control mechanisms. As we reported last September, tax expenditures represent a significant commitment and are not typically subjected to review or reexamination.

Mandatory spending programs—like tax expenditures—are governed by eligibility rules and benefit formulas, which means that funds are spent as required to provide benefits to those who are eligible and wish to participate. Since Congress and the President must change substantive law to change the cost of these programs, they are relatively uncontrollable on an annual basis. Moreover, as we reported in a 1994 analysis, their cost cannot be controlled by the same "spending cap" mechanism used for discretionary spending.[3]

By their very nature mandatories limit budget flexibility.[4] As figure 1 shows, mandatory spending has grown as a share of the total federal budget. For example, mandatory spending has grown from 27 percent before the creation of Medicare and Medicaid to 42 percent in 1985 to 54 percent last year. (Total spending not subject to annual appropriations—mandatory spending and net interest—has grown from 56 percent in 1985 to 61 percent last year.) Under both the Congressional Budget Office baseline estimates and the President's Budget, this spending would grow further.

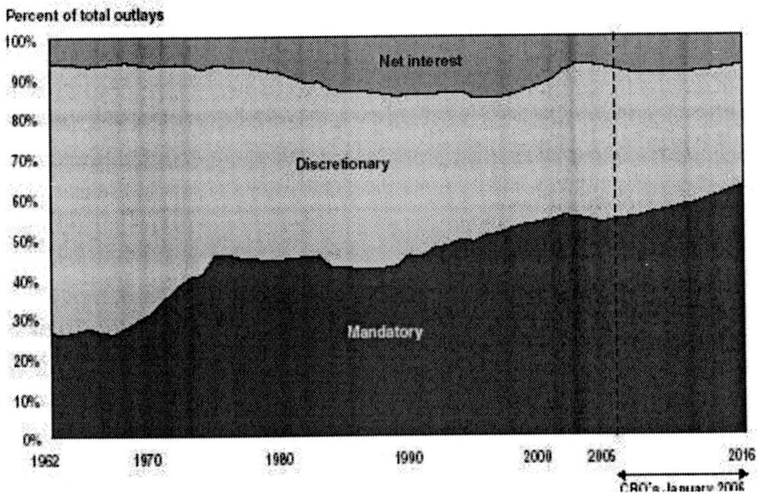

Source: OMB and CBO.
Note: Projections assume discretionary spending grows with inflation after 2006.

Figure 1. Federal Spending for Mandatory and Discretionary Programs

While the long-term fiscal outlook is driven by Medicare, Medicaid and Social Security, it does not mean that all other mandatory programs should be "given a pass." As we have noted elsewhere, reexamination of the "fit" between government programs and the needs and priorities of the nation should be an accepted practice.[5] So in terms of budget flexibility—the freedom of each Congress and President to allocate public resources—we cannot ignore mandatory spending programs even if they do not drive the aggregate.

While some might suggest that mandatory programs could be controlled by being converted to discretionary or annually appropriated programs, that seems unlikely to happen. If we look across the range of mandatories we see many programs have objectives and missions that contribute to the achievement of a range of broad-based and important public policy goals such as providing a floor of income security in retirement, fighting hunger, fostering higher education, and providing access to affordable health care. To these ends, these programs—and tax expenditures—were designed to provide benefits automatically to those who take the desired action or meet the specified eligibility criteria without subjecting them to an annual decision regarding spending or delay in the provision of benefits such a process might entail.

Although mandatory spending is not amenable to "caps," that does not mean that mandatory programs should be permitted to be on autopilot and grow to an unlimited extent. Since the spending for any given entitlement or other mandatory program is a function of the interaction between the eligibility rules and the benefit formula—either or both of which may incorporate exogenous factors such as economic downturns—the way to change the path of spending for any of these programs is to change those rules or formulas. We recently issued a report on "triggers"—some measure which, when reached or exceeded, would prompt a response connected to that program.[6] By identifying significant increases in the spending path of a mandatory program relatively early and acting to constrain it, Congress may avert much larger and potentially disruptive financial challenges and program changes in the future.

A trigger is a measure and a signal mechanism—like an alarm clock. It could trigger a "soft" response—one that calls attention to the growth rate or the level of spending and prompts special consideration when the threshold or target is breached. Two examples of soft responses that could be triggered include requiring the relevant agency to prepare a report analyzing why the trigger was tripped and/or requiring the President to submit a proposal to change the path or explain why he thinks it should remain unchanged. The Medicare program already contains a "soft" response trigger: The President is required to submit a proposal for action to Congress if the Medicare Trustees determine in 2 consecutive years that the general revenue share of Medicare spending is projected to exceed 45 percent during a 7-year period.[7] Each year the Social Security and Medicare Trustees test for program financial adequacy over the next 10 years. The results of the test are included in the respective Trustees' reports to Congress, in which they note that failure to meet this test is an indication that action is needed. A few Social Security reform proposals have taken this further by including language requiring Presidential and Congressional action if the Social Security Board of Trustees determines that the balance ratio of either of the Social Security trust funds will be zero for any calendar year during the succeeding 75 years.[8] Given the complexity and controversy associated with reforming entitlements, commissions might be one means to come up with possible triggers appropriate to the specific programs.

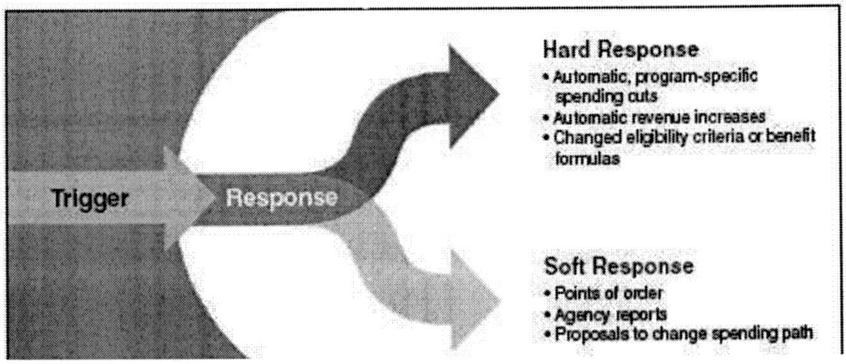

Source: GAO analysis.

Figure 2. Conceptual Differences between Hard and Soft Responses

Soft responses can help in alerting decision makers of potential problems but they do not ensure that action to decrease spending or increase revenue is taken. With soft responses, the fiscal path continues unless Congress and the President take action. In contrast, a trigger could lead to "hard" responses requiring a predetermined, program-specific action to take place, such as changes in eligibility criteria and benefit formulas, automatic revenue increases, or automatic spending cuts. With hard responses, spending is automatically constrained, revenue is automatically increased, or both, unless Congress takes action to override. For example, this year the President's Budget proposes to change the Medicare trigger from solely "soft" to providing a "hard" (automatic) response if Congress fails to enact the President's proposal.[9] Figure 2 below illustrates the conceptual differences between hard and soft responses of a budget trigger.

In our recent report on mandatory spending triggers, we discussed the kinds of responses that might be triggered and the importance of program-specific design. Proposed changes in underlying benefits structure and design of a mandatory program can be considered in the context both of the factors that drive the growth of that program and the specific goals and objectives of the program. For example, some mandatories are intended to have a countercyclical effect; any triggered response in these programs would have to be designed not to interfere with that function. Its design, therefore, would have to be sensitive to whether growth comes because the program is, in fact, working as an automatic stabilizer.

Both near- and long-term perspectives should be considered in the design of triggers. For some programs, it might be appropriate to tie the trigger to historical data—for example, to see whether spending growth was greater than some historical average or path. For programs that expose the government to long-term commitments, it might be more appropriate to tie the trigger to projections of future spending. For "contributory" programs that represent a long-term commitment of future earmarked resources, such as Social Security, one appropriate measure could be the actuarial projections of the 75-year outlook. Some similar approach might be used for programs like pension or health insurance.

Any discussion to create triggered responses and their design must recognize that unlike controls on discretionary spending, there is some tension between the idea of triggers and the nature of entitlement and other mandatory spending programs. These programs—as with tax provisions such as tax expenditures—were designed to provide benefits based on eligibility formulas or actions as opposed to an annual decision regarding spending. This tension makes it more challenging to constrain costs and to design both triggers and triggered responses. At the same time, with only about one-third of the budget under the control of the annual appropriations process, considering ways to increase transparency, oversight, and control of mandatory programs must be part of addressing the nation's long-term fiscal challenges.

Before I turn to the largest driver of our long-term challenge—rising health care costs—let me note that the idea of triggers need not only apply to spending. The revenue side of the budget should also be addressed. If, for example, one option to cover the increased costs of a mandatory spending program was a premium increase or tax increase, it would serve to increase public visibility and could make the American people more aware of how much they are paying for services. More directly analogous to mandatory spending programs is the extensive use of tax incentives, rather than direct spending authority, to address various social objectives. As we reported in September 2005,[10] the sum of revenue loss estimates associated with tax expenditures—such as tax exclusions, credits, and deductions—was nearly $730 billion in 2004.[11] Under the most recent estimates, this has risen to more than $775 billion in 2005.

Let me be clear that in suggesting application of this analysis to tax expenditures I am not addressing the appropriate level of taxation as a share of GDP. Whatever level of revenue is deemed appropriate, tax expenditures that seek to achieve programmatic or policy goals should—like other federal programs or activities—be reviewed to determine their effectiveness, continued relevance, affordability, and sustainability. Tax expenditures have a significant effect on overall tax rates—in that, for any given level of revenue, overall tax rates must be higher to offset the revenue forgone through tax expenditures—as well as the budget and fiscal flexibility. They also contribute to the growing complexity of the federal tax system. Many tax expenditures operate like mandatory spending programs and generally are not subject to reauthorization. Such tax expenditures are embedded in the tax system. They are not subject to a performance test and are off the radar screen for the most part. This is a concern from a budgetary standpoint because taxpayer dollars committed to fund these expenditures do not compete in the annual appropriations process and are effectively "fully funded" before any discretionary spending is considered. The analysis we have applied to spending would also be useful in examining tax expenditures.

Federal Health Care Spending Drives the Long-Term Fiscal Challenge

Among mandatory spending programs—and indeed tax expenditures—the health area is especially important because the long-term fiscal challenge is largely a health care challenge. Contrary to public perceptions, health care is the biggest driver of the long-term fiscal challenge. While Social Security is important because of its size, health care spending is both large and projected to grow much more rapidly.

Our most recent simulation results illustrate the importance of health care in the long-term fiscal outlook as well as the imperative to take action. Simply put, our nation's fiscal policy is on an imprudent and unsustainable course. These long-term budget simulations show, as do those published last December by the Congressional Budget Office (CBO),[12] that over the long term we face a large and growing structural deficit due primarily to known demographic trends and rising health care costs and lower federal revenues as a percentage of the economy. Continuing on this unsustainable fiscal path will gradually erode, if not suddenly damage, our economy, our standard of living, and ultimately our national security. Our current path also will increasingly constrain our ability to address emerging and unexpected budgetary needs and increase the burdens that will be faced by future generations.

Figures 3 and 4 present our long-term simulations under two different sets of assumptions. In figure 3, we start with CBO's 10-year baseline—constructed according to the statutory requirements for that baseline.[13] Consistent with these requirements, discretionary spending is assumed to grow with inflation for the first 10 years and tax cuts scheduled to expire are assumed to expire. After 2016, discretionary spending is assumed to grow with the economy, and revenue is held

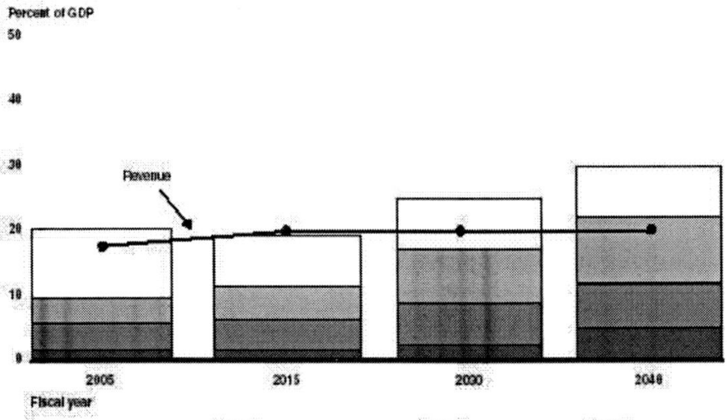

Source: GAO's January 2006 analysis.

Note: In addition to the expiration of tax cuts, revenue as a share of GDP increases through 2016 due to (1) real bracket creep, (2) more taxpayers becoming subject to the alternative minimum tax (AMT), and (3) increased revenue from tax-deferred retirement accounts. After 2016, revenue as a share of GDP is held constant.

Figure 3. Composition of Spending as a Share of GDP under Baseline Extended

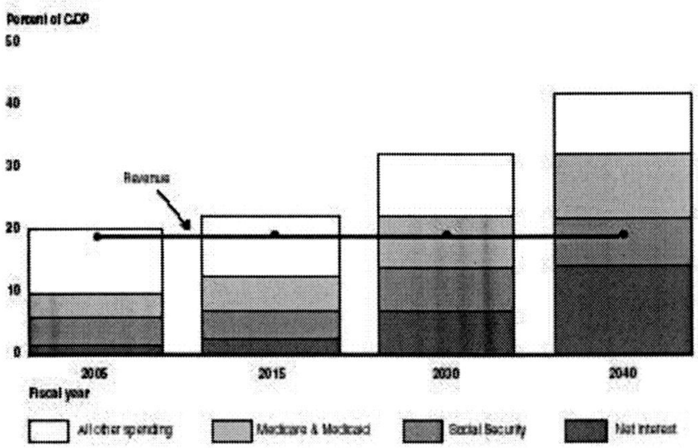

Source: GAO's January 2006 analysis.

Note: This includes certain tax provisions that expired at the end of 2005, such as the increased AMT exemption amount.

Figure 4. Composition of Spending as a Share of GDP Assuming Discretionary Spending Grows with GDP after 2006 and All Expiring Tax Provisions Are Extended

constant as a share of GDP at the 2016 level. In figure 4, two assumptions are changed: (1) discretionary spending is assumed to grow with the economy after 2006 rather than merely with inflation, and (2) all expiring tax provisions are extended. For both simulations, Social Security and Medicare spending is based on the 2005 Trustees' intermediate projections, and we assume that benefits continue to be paid in full after the trust funds are exhausted. Medicaid spending is based on CBO's December 2005 long-term projections under mid-range assumptions.

As these simulations illustrate, absent significant policy changes on the spending and/or revenue side of the budget, the growth in mandatory spending on federal retirement and especially health entitlements will encumber an escalating share of the government's resources. Indeed, when we assume that all the temporary tax reductions are made permanent and discretionary spending keeps pace with the economy, our long-term simulations suggest that by 2040 federal revenues may be adequate to pay only some Social Security benefits and interest on the federal debt. Neither slowing the growth in discretionary spending nor allowing the tax provisions to expire—nor both together—would eliminate the imbalance. Although revenues will be part of the debate about our fiscal future, assuming no changes to Social Security, Medicare, Medicaid, and other drivers of the long-term fiscal gap would require at least a doubling of taxes—and that seems highly implausible. Economic growth is essential, but we will not be able to simply grow our way out of the problem. The numbers speak loudly: our projected fiscal gap is simply too great. Closing the current long-term fiscal gap would require sustained economic growth far beyond that experienced in U.S. economic history since World War II. Tough choices are inevitable, and the sooner we act the better.

Accordingly, substantive reform of the major health programs and Social Security is critical to recapturing our future fiscal flexibility. Ultimately, the nation will have to decide what level of federal benefits and spending it wants and how it will pay for these benefits. Our current fiscal path will increasingly constrain our ability to address emerging and unexpected budgetary needs and increase the burdens that will be faced by future generations. Continuing on this path will mean escalating and ultimately unsustainable federal deficits and debt that will serve to threaten our future national security as well as the standard of living for the American people.

The aging population and rising health care spending will have significant implications not only for the budget, but also the economy as a whole. Figure 5 shows the total future draw on the economy represented by Social Security, Medicare, and Medicaid. Under the 2005 Trustees' intermediate estimates and

CBO's 2005 long-term Medicaid estimates under mid-range assumptions, spending for these entitlement programs combined will grow to 15.7 percent of gross domestic product (GDP) in 2030 from today's 8.4 percent. It is clear that, taken together, Social Security, Medicare, and Medicaid represent an unsustainable burden on future generations.

Furthermore, most of the long-term growth is in health care. While Social Security in its current form will grow from 4.3 percent of GDP today to 6.4 percent in 2080, Medicare's burden on the economy will quintuple—from 2.7 percent to 13.8 percent of the economy—and these projections assume a growth rate for Medicare spending that is below historical experience! As figure 5 shows, unlike Social Security which grows larger as a share of the economy and then levels off, within this projection period we do not see Medicare growth abating. Whether or not the President's Budget proposals on Medicare are adopted, they should serve to raise public awareness of the importance of health care costs to both today's budget and tomorrow's. This could serve to jump start a discussion about appropriate ways to control the major driver of our long-term fiscal outlook—health care spending.

As noted, unlike Social Security, Medicare spending growth rates reflect not only a burgeoning beneficiary population, but also the escalation of health care costs at rates well exceeding general rates of inflation. The growth of medical technology has contributed to increases in the number and quality of health care services. Moreover, the actual costs of health care consumption are not transparent. Consumers are largely insulated by third-party payers from the cost of health care decisions.

The health care spending problem is particularly vexing for the federal budget, affecting not only Medicare and Medicaid but also other important federal health programs, such as for our military personnel and veterans. For example, Department of Defense health care spending rose from about $12 billion in 1990 to about $30.4 billion in 2004—in part, to meet additional demand resulting from program eligibility expansions for military retirees, reservists, and the dependents of those two groups and for the increased needs of active duty personnel involved in conflicts in Iraq, Bosnia, and Afghanistan. Expenditures by the Department of Veterans Affairs have also grown—from about $12 billion in 1990 to about $26.8 billion in 2004—as an increasing number of veterans look to federal programs to supply their health care needs.

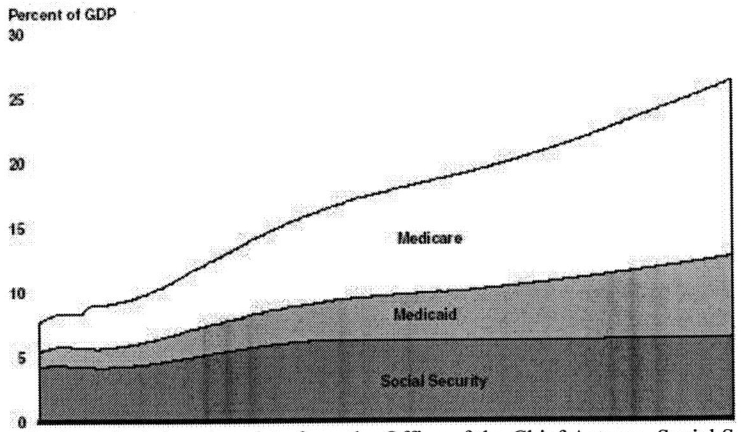

Source: GAO analysis based on data from the Office of the Chief Actuary, Social Security Administration, Office of the Actuary,Centers for Medicare and Medicaid Services, and the Congressional Budget Office.

Note: Social Security and Medicare projections are based on the intermediate assumptions of the 2005 Trustees' Reports. Medicaid projections are based on CBO's January 2006 short-term Medicaid estimates and CBO's December 2005 long-term Medicaid projections under mid-range assumptions.

Figure 5. Social Security, Medicare, and Medicaid Spending as a Percent of GDP

The challenge to rein in health care spending is not limited to public payers, however, as the phenomenon of rising health care costs associated with new technology exists system-wide. This means that addressing the unsustainability of health care costs is also a major competitiveness and societal challenge that calls for us as a nation to fundamentally rethink how we define, deliver, and finance health care in both the public and the private sectors. A major difficulty is that our current system does little to encourage informed discussions and decisions about the costs and value of various health care services. These decisions are very important when it comes to cutting-edge drugs and medical technologies, which can be incredibly expensive but only marginally better than other alternatives. As a nation, we are going to need to weigh unlimited individual wants against broader societal needs and decide how responsibility for financing health care should be divided among employers, individuals, and government. Ultimately, we may need to define a set of basic and essential health care services to which every American is ensured access. Individuals wanting additional services, and insurance coverage to pay for them, might be required to allocate their own resources. Clearly, such a dramatic change would require a long transition period—all the more reason to act sooner rather than later.

- Develop a set of national practice standards to help avoid unnecessary care, improve outcomes, and reduce litigation.
- Encourage case management approaches for people with expensive acute and chronic conditions to improve the quality and efficiency of care delivered and avoid inappropriate care.
- Foster the use of information technology to increase consistency, transparency, and accountability in health care.
- Emphasize prevention and wellness care, including nutrition.
- Leverage the government's purchasing power to control costs for prescription drugs and other health care services.
- Revise certain federal tax preferences for health care to encourage the more efficient use of appropriate care.
- Create an insurance market that adequately pools risk and offers alternative levels of coverage.
- Develop a core set of basic and essential services with supplemental coverage being available as an option but at a cost. Use the Federal Employees Health Benefits Program (FEHBP) model as a possible means to experiment and see the way forward.
- Limit spending growth for government-sponsored health care programs (e.g., percentage of the budget and/or the economy).

Source: GAO

Figure 6. Selected Reforms Aimed at Moderating Health Care Spending

In recent years, policy analysts have discussed a number of incremental reforms that take aim at moderating health care spending, in part by unmasking health care's true costs. (See figure 6 for a list of selected reforms.) Among these reforms is to devise additional cost-sharing provisions to make health care costs more transparent to patients. Currently, many insured individuals pay relatively little out of pocket for care at the point of delivery because of comprehensive health care coverage—precluding the opportunity to sensitize these patients to the cost of their care.

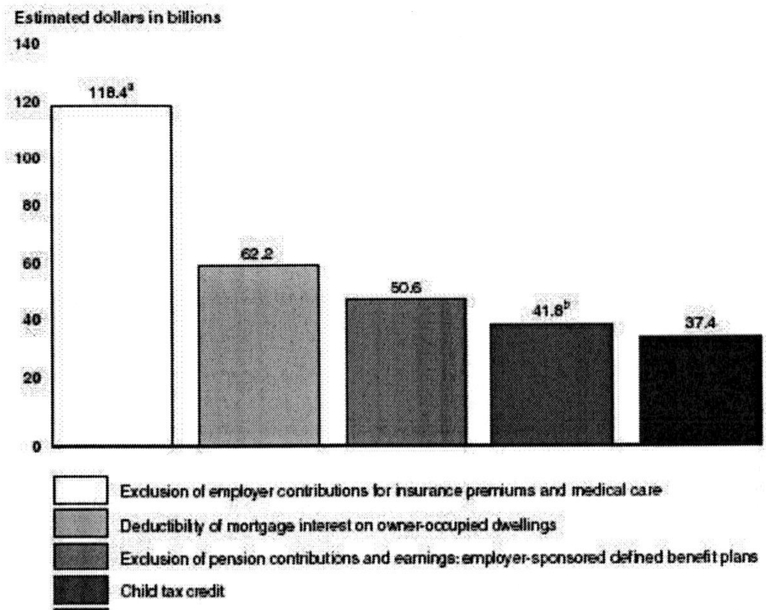

Source: Office of Management and Budget (OMB), *Analytical Perspectives, Budget of the United States Government, Fiscal Year 2007.*

Note: "Tax expenditures" refers to the special tax provisions that are contained in the federal income taxes on individuals and corporations. OMB does not include forgone revenue from other federal taxes such as Social Security and Medicare payroll taxes.

[a]If the payroll tax exclusion were also counted here, the total tax expenditure for employer contributions for health insurance premiums would be about 50 percent higher or $177.6 billion.

[b]This is the revenue loss and does not include associated outlays of $14.6 billion.

Figure 7. Health Care Was the Nation's Top Tax Expenditure in Fiscal Year 2005

Other steps include reforming the policies that give tax preferences to insured individuals and their employers. These policies permit the value of employees' health insurance premiums to be excluded from the calculation of their taxable earnings and exclude the value of the premium from the employers' calculation of payroll taxes for both themselves and employees. Tax preferences also exist for health savings accounts and other consumer-directed plans. These tax exclusions represent a significant source of forgone federal revenue and work at cross-purposes to the goal of moderating health care spending. As figure 7 shows, in 2005 the tax expenditure responsible for the greatest revenue loss was that for the exclusion of employer contributions for employees' insurance premiums and medical care.

Another area conducive to incremental change involves provider payment reforms. These reforms are intended to induce physicians, hospitals, and other health care providers to improve on quality and efficiency. For example, studies of Medicare patients in different geographic areas have found that despite receiving a greater volume of care, patients in higher use areas did not have better health outcomes or experience greater satisfaction with care than those living in lower use areas. Public and private payers are experimenting with payment reforms designed to foster the delivery of care that is proven to be both clinically and cost effective. Ideally, identifying and rewarding efficient providers and encouraging inefficient providers to emulate best practices will result in better value for the dollars spent on care. The development of uniform standards of practice could lead to ensuring that people with chronic illnesses, a small but expensive population, received more and cost-effective and patient-centered care while reducing unwarranted medical malpractice litigation.

The problem of escalating health care costs is complex because addressing federal programs such as Medicare and the federal-state Medicaid program will need to involve change in the health care system of which they are a part—not just within federal programs. This will be a major societal challenge that will affect all age groups. Because our health care system is complex, with multiple interrelated pieces, solutions to health care cost growth are likely to be incremental and require a number of extensive efforts over many years. In my view, taking steps to address the health care cost dilemma system-wide puts us on the right path for correcting the long-term fiscal problems posed by the nation's health care entitlements.

I have focused today on health care because it is a driver of our fiscal outlook. Indeed, health care is already putting a squeeze on the federal budget.

Health care is the dominant but not the only driver of our long-term fiscal challenge. Today it is hard to think of our fiscal imbalances as a big problem: the economy is healthy and interest rates seem low. We, however, have an obligation to look beyond today. Budgets, deficits, and long-term fiscal and economic outlooks are not just about numbers: they are also about values. It is time for all of us to recognize our stewardship obligation for the future. We should act sooner rather than later. We all must make choices that may be difficult and unpleasant today to avoid passing an even greater burden on to future generations. Let us not be the generation who sent the bill for its consumption to its children and grandchildren.

Thank you Mr. Chairman, Mr. Spratt, and members of the Committee for having me today. We at GAO, of course, stand ready to assist you and your colleagues as you tackle these important challenges.

End Notes

[1] Tax expenditures result in forgone revenue for the federal government due to preferential provisions in the tax code, such as exemptions and exclusions from taxation, deductions, credits, deferral of tax liability, and preferential tax rates. These tax expenditures are often aimed at policy goals similar to those of federal spending programs; existing tax expenditures, for example, are intended to encourage economic development in disadvantaged areas, finance postsecondary education, and stimulate research and development. See GAO, *Government Performance and Accountability: Tax Expenditures Represent a Substantial Federal Commitment and Need to Be Reexamined,* GAO-05-690 (Washington, D.C.: Sept. 23, 2005).

[2] GAO, *21st Century Challenges: Reexamining the Base of the Federal Government*, GAO-05-325SP (Washington, D.C.: February 2005).

[3] GAO, *Budget Policy: Issues in Capping Mandatory Spending*, GAO/AIMD-94-155 (Washington, D.C.: July 18, 1994).

[4] Similarly tax expenditures may limit flexibility on the revenue side; there is a tradeoff between tax rates and revenue lost through tax expenditures. In order to raise a given amount of federal revenue, tax rates must be raised higher than they otherwise need to be due to revenue losses from tax expenditures.

[5] GAO-05-325SP.

[6] GAO, *Mandatory Spending: Using Budget Triggers to Constrain Growth*, GAO-06-276 (Washington, D.C.: Jan. 31, 2006).

[7] For the purpose of the Medicare trigger, general revenue is defined as the difference between Medicare program outlays and dedicated Medicare financing sources. Dedicated Medicare financing sources are defined as Hospital Insurance (HI) payroll taxes, the HI share of income taxes on Social Security benefits, state transfers for Part D prescription drug benefits, premiums paid under Parts A, B, and D, and any gifts received by the trust funds.

[8] Recently, this provision was included in the Bipartisan Retirement Security Act of 2005, H.R. 440, 109th Cong. § 14 (2005).

[9] The response now would include a sequester if the Congress did not act on the President's proposal. The proposed sequester would result in a four-tenths of a percent reduction in all payments to providers beginning in the year the threshold is exceeded. Each year the shortfall continues to occur the reduction would grow by an additional four-tenths of a percent. We have not yet analyzed how this would work.

[10] See GAO-05-690.

[11] Summing the individual tax expenditure estimates is useful for gauging the general magnitude of the federal revenue involved, but it does not take into account possible interactions between individual provisions.

[12] CBO, *The Long-Term Budget Outlook* (Washington, D.C.: December 2005).

[13] CBO, *The Budget and Economic Outlook: Fiscal Years 2007 to 2016* (Washington, D.C.: January 2006).

In: Federal Spending: A Riddle Wrapped ...
Editor: Frederick C. Hargis
ISBN: 978-1-60741-728-6
2010 Nova Science Publishers, Inc.

Chapter 3

MANDATORY SPENDING SINCE 1962

Andrew Austin and Mindy R. Levit

ABSTRACT

This chapter reviews trends in mandatory spending since 1962 and discusses CBO baseline projections of mandatory spending, which extend to 2018. The report examines mandatory spending's growth relative to total federal spending and to the size of the U.S. economy, and looks at how the composition of mandatory spending has changed.

SUMMARY

Federal spending is often divided into three categories: discretionary spending, mandatory spending, and net interest. Mandatory spending includes federal government spending on entitlement programs and Food Stamps as well as other budget outlays controlled by laws other than appropriation acts. Entitlement programs such as Social Security and Medicare make up the bulk of mandatory spending. Other mandatory spending programs include Temporary Assistance for Needy Families (TANF), Supplemental Security Income (SSI), unemployment insurance, some veterans' benefits, federal employee retirement and disability, Food Stamps, and the earned income tax credit (EITC). Discretionary spending is provided and controlled through appropriations acts.

Mandatory spending accounts for over half of total federal spending and almost a ninth of gross domestic product (GDP). Social Security accounts for over a fifth of federal spending. Medicare and the federal share of Medicaid, the fastest growing components of mandatory spending, together account for over a fifth of federal spending. Those three programs, therefore, make up over 40% of federal spending.

The composition of mandatory spending has changed significantly over the past 40 years. In 1962, before the 1965 creation of Medicare and Medicaid, mandatory spending was less than 30% of all federal spending. At that time, Social Security accounted for about half of all mandatory spending. By 2008, mandatory spending composed 54% of total federal spending. Medicare and Medicaid grew from almost nothing in 1965 to about 4.6% of GDP in 2008. Similarly, Social Security grew from 2.5% of GDP in 1962 to 4.3% in 2008. SSI outlays have remained between 0.2% and 0.3% of GDP.

Federal spending has outrun federal revenues for the last six years. In the long term, projections suggest that if current policies remain unchanged, the United States faces a major fiscal imbalance, largely due to rising health care costs and impending Baby Boomer retirements. Over the next 75 years, growth in Medicare and Medicaid is projected to be the largest contributor to the long-term fiscal shortfall. Medicare and the federal portion of Medicaid spending is projected to expand from 4.6% of GDP in 2008 to 18.5% in 2082 according to a Congressional Budget Office (CBO) extended baseline projection. Social Security is projected to grow from 4.3% of GDP in 2008 to 6.4% of GDP by 2082. Thus, funding health care costs while the U.S. population ages promises to strain federal budgets in coming decades.

Because discretionary spending is now at a historic low as a proportion of total federal outlays, some budget experts contend that any significant reductions in federal spending must include cuts in entitlement spending. Other budget and social policy experts contend that cuts in entitlement spending could compromise their goals: the economic security of the elderly and the poor. Proposals for fundamental reform may strive to ease long-term fiscal strains while preserving the social protection goals of these programs.

OVERVIEW

Mandatory spending includes federal government spending on entitlement programs and Food Stamps as well as other budget outlays controlled by laws other than appropriation acts. Entitlement programs such as Social Security and Medicare make up the bulk of mandatory spending. Congress sets eligibility requirements and benefits for entitlement programs, rather than appropriating a fixed sum each year. Therefore, if the eligibility requirements are met for a specific mandatory program, outlays are made automatically. Other mandatory spending programs include Temporary Assistance for Needy Families (TANF), Supplemental Security Income (SSI), unemployment insurance, certain veterans' benefits, federal employee retirement and disability, Food Stamps, and the earned income tax credit (EITC). Mandatory spending also includes many smaller budgetary items, such as salaries of Members of Congress, the President, and federal judges.

In FY2008, mandatory spending—totaling 11.2% of gross domestic product (GDP)— overshadowed discretionary spending's 7.9% share of GDP. In addition, federal net interest payments accounted for 1.7% of GDP. That is, over half of all federal spending in FY2008 (total federal spending represented 20.9% of GDP) was spent on mandatory programs. The Congressional Budget Office (CBO) projects that mandatory spending will continue to account for over half of all federal outlays in the coming decade. Mandatory spending, according to CBO current-law projections, will be about 60% of total spending in 2018.

The federal government spends more on mandatory items than on discretionary items. Mandatory spending was 54% of federal spending in 2008. Discretionary spending in 2008 totaled just under 40% and net interest payments accounted for the remaining portion of spending. Social Security, Medicare, and the federal share of Medicaid alone composed over 40% of all federal spending. Social Security outlays in 2008 were 38.6% of mandatory spending and income support programs accounted for 14.4% of mandatory spending.

Mandatory spending plays a major role in larger fiscal trends. During the 1950s and 1960s, federal deficits were relatively small and (except for two years) below 2% of GDP. The total federal deficit jumped from 1.2% of GDP in FY2007 to 3.2% of GDP in FY2008, in large part due to financial turmoil and a recession. During economic downturns, government revenues fall and expenditures rise as more people become eligible for mandatory programs such as unemployment insurance and income support programs, causing deficits to increase or surpluses to shrink. These effects, known as "automatic stabilizers," provide a countercyclical fiscal stimulus in the short run without the need for new legislative action.

This chapter reviews trends in mandatory spending since 1962. CBO baseline projections of mandatory spending, which extend to 2018, as well as extended baseline projections through 2082 are used to consider the long-term consequences of current mandatory spending policies.[1] The report looks at mandatory spending and how it has grown over time relative to total federal spending and to the size of the U.S. economy.

WHAT DOES MANDATORY SPENDING INCLUDE?

Mandatory spending is controlled by laws other than appropriations acts. Such laws usually specify an obligation on the part of the federal government to spend funds for certain purposes. In most cases, the authorizing law requires, in the form of an eligibility criteria and a benefit formula, payment to an individual or entity (e.g., a state). Mandatory spending typically is provided in permanent or multi-year appropriations contained in the authorizing law, and therefore, the funding becomes available automatically each year, without legislative action by Congress. In contrast, discretionary spending is provided and controlled through the annual appropriations process.[2] Net interest payments, which are automatically authorized, are often reported as a separate category.

A portion of entitlement spending, such as for Medicaid and certain veterans' programs, is funded in annual appropriations acts. Such entitlement spending is referred to as appropriated entitlements. The level of spending for appropriated entitlements, like other entitlements, is based on the benefit and eligibility criteria established in law. The amount of budget authority provided in appropriations acts for these specific programs is based on meeting projected spending levels. Since the authorizing legislation effectively determines the amount of budget authority required, the Budget Enforcement Act (BEA) of 1990 (P.L. 101-508) classified appropriated entitlement spending as mandatory.[3]

Not all mandatory spending funds entitlement programs. For example, the Forest Service makes some payments to states that are mandatory, but are not entitlements. Some agencies gained authority to sign contracts or create obligations in other ways, which GAO has termed "backdoor" spending authority.[4] Those obligations become part of mandatory spending unless limited by the BEA or other budget legislation. As noted above, salaries of Members of Congress, the President, and federal judges are also deemed mandatory.

Mandatory spending is offset by certain fees and payments, which are counted as offsetting receipts rather than as revenue. Market-like charges, such as Medicare Part A deductibles and Medicare Part B premiums, are considered offsetting receipts. Some intragovernmental transfers, such as agency rents paid to the General Services Administration (GSA), are also counted as offsetting receipts by the recipient agency. Payments by Medicare beneficiaries and the federal government's tax and pension contributions in its role as an employer comprise the largest component of offsetting receipts within the mandatory spending category.

Table 1. Mandatory Spending in Detail

	FY2008 (Estimated)			**FY2018 (Baseline Projection)**		
Category	**$ Billions**	**% of Mandatory Spending[a]**	**% of GDP**	**$Billions**	**% of Mandatory Spending[a]**	**% of GDP**
Social Security	612	38.6%	4.3%	1,114	40.2%	5.0%
Medicare[b]	454	28.6%	3.2%	889	32.1%	4.0%
Medicaid	202	12.8%	1.4%	449	16.2%	2.0%
Income Security	**228**	**14.4%**	**1.6%**	**268**	**9.7%**	**1.2%**
SSI	41	2.6%	0.3%	55	2.0%	0.2%
EITC and child tax credits	58 3.6%	0.4%	45	1.6%	0.2%	
Unemployment comp.	44	2.8%	0.3%	56	2.0%	0.3%
Food Stamps	39	2.4%	0.3%	54	2.0%	0.2%
Family support	25	1.6%	0.2%	26	0.9%	0.1%
Child nutrition	15	0.9%	0.1%	23	0.8%	0.1%
Foster care	7	0.4%	0.0%	9	0.3%	0.0%
Civilian and Military Retirement	**130**	**8.2%**	**0.9%**	**187**	**6.8%**	**0.8%**
Federal civilian	75	4.7%	0.5%	114	4.1%	0.5%
Military	46	2.9%	0.3%	62	2.3%	0.3%
Other	9	0.6%	0.1%	11	0.4%	0.0%
Veterans	**45**	**2.8%**	**0.3%**	**66**	**2.4%**	**0.3%**
Income Security	41	2.6%	0.3%	53	1.9%	0.2%
Other	3	0.2%	0.0%	13	0.5%	0.1%
Other Programs	**116**	**7.3%**	**0.8%**	**82**	**2.9%**	**0.4%**
Agriculture	14	0.9%	0.1%	15	0.5%	0.1%
TRICARE For Life	8	0.5%	0.1%	15	0.5%	0.1%

Table 1 (Continued)

Category	FY2008 (Estimated) $ Billions	FY2008 % of Mandatory Spending[a]	FY2008 % of GDP	FY2018 (Baseline Projection) $Billions	FY2018 % of Mandatory Spending[a]	FY2018 % of GDP
Student loans	4	0.3%	0.0%	3	0.1%	0.0%
SCHIP	7	0.4%	0.0%	5	0.2%	0.0%
Social services	5	0.3%	0.0%	6	0.2%	0.0%
Refundable income tax rebates	38	2.4%	0.3%	0	0.0%	0.0%
Deposit insurance	14	0.9%	0.1%	-5	-0.2%	0.0%
Other	24	1.6%	0.2%	43	1.5%	0.2%
Offsetting Receipts	**-201**	**-12.7%**	**-1.4%**	**-285**	**-10.3%**	**-1.3%**
Medicare	-69	-4.3%	-0.5%	-128	-4.6%	-0.6%
Employer's share of employee retirement	-52	-3.3%	-0.4%	-80	-2.9%	-0.4%
Other	-81	-5.1%	-0.6%	-78	-2.8%	-0.3%
Total Mandatory Spending	**1,586**	**100%**	**11.2%**	**2,770**	**100%**	**12.5%**
Medicare Spending Net of Offsetting Receipts	385	24.3%	2.70%	761	27.50%	3.4%
Net Interest	**244**	**15.4%**	**1.7%**	**396**	**14.3%**	**1.8%**

Source: CBO report "*The Budget and Economic Outlook: An Update*," Sept. 2008, Table 1-4. See source for notes. Some items do not sum to totals due to rounding.

a. Denominator includes offsetting receipts.

b. Excludes offsetting receipts.

Table 1 presents components of projected mandatory spending in 2008 and CBO baseline projections for mandatory spending in FY2018.

MANDATORY SPENDING TRENDS OVER TIME

Mandatory spending has taken up a larger and larger share of the federal budget over time. Mandatory spending, minuscule before the Great Depression, grew over time with enactment of the Social Security Act of 1935 (P.L. 74-271) and a generation later with the Medicare Act of 1965 (P.L. 89-97).[5] In 1962, three years before the creation of Medicare and Medicaid, less than 30% of all federal spending was mandatory. At that time, Social Security accounted for about half of all mandatory spending.[6] In the mid-1970s, growth of mandatory spending as a share of total federal spending slowed. Since then, mandatory spending has increased its share of federal spending at a gradual pace.

Figure 1 shows mandatory spending since 1962 and CBO baseline projections for these components to 2018, both expressed as a percentage of total federal spending. Mandatory spending was about a quarter of total federal spending in 1962 (nearly a third if offsetting receipts are excluded). In 1968, mandatory spending began growing relative to total federal spending and by 1975 accounted for about 45% of total spending (about half before offsetting receipts). From the mid-1980s through 1990, mandatory spending's share in total spending remained relatively steady, before starting to grow again after 1990. In 2008, mandatory spending accounted for 53.7% of total spending (or 60% before offsetting receipts).

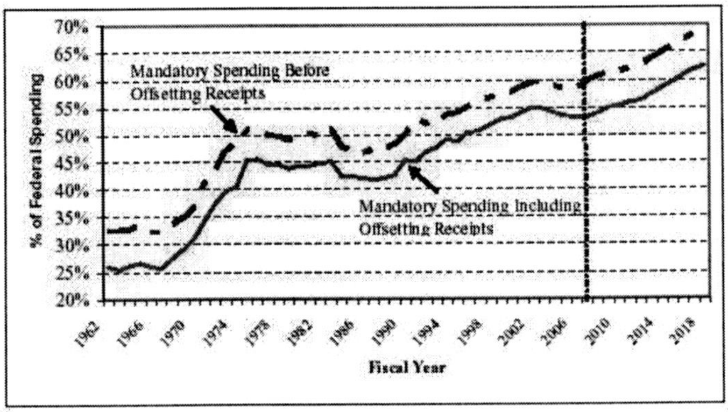

Source: CBO historical tables. CBO treats some offsetting receipts, especially regarding Medicare, differently than OMB. CBO baseline projections to the right of dotted line.

Figure 1. Mandatory Spending and Offsetting Receipts As a Percentage of Total Federal Spending

Mandatory spending plays a major role in larger fiscal trends. During the 1950s and 1960s, federal deficits were relatively small and below 2% of GDP (except for two years). While the FY2007 deficit was 1.2% of GDP, the FY2008 deficit was 3.2% in large part due to financial turmoil and a recession. During economic downturns, government revenues fall and expenditures rise as more people qualify for unemployment insurance and income support programs, causing deficits to increase or surpluses to shrink. These effects, known as "automatic stabilizers," provide a countercyclical stimulus in the short run without the need for new legislative action.

Discretionary spending as a share of total federal expenditures has fallen for several reasons. First, defense spending generally has taken a smaller share of the federal budget since World War II, despite recent increases in military spending. Second, budget limits or "caps" in the 1990s held down discretionary spending, and so discretionary spending fell as a proportion of total federal spending. Third, rising mandatory spending has decreased discretionary spending's share in total federal spending.

Changes in the Composition of Mandatory Spending

The composition of mandatory spending has changed dramatically over the past 40 years and, according to CBO baseline projections, will to continue to change over the decade. **Figure 2** shows how major components of mandatory spending have evolved since 1962.

Persistent increases in health care spending have been a particularly important driver of mandatory spending trends. Indigent health care programs, before the 1965 Medicare Act folded them into Medicaid, accounted for less than 0.5% of mandatory spending. Since enactment of the 1965 Medicare Act, the Medicare and Medicaid programs have composed a growing share of mandatory spending. Medicare and Medicaid spending grew from 15.5% of mandatory spending in 1970 to 41.4% in 2008. CBO baseline projections show further increases in federal health spending will cause the Medicaid and Medicare share of andatory spending to continue to rise. As an example, by 2018, based on CBO baseline projections, Medicare is projected to account for 32.1% of mandatory spending and Medicaid is projected to account for an additional 16.2%.

In contrast to growing per capita health care spending, Social Security's share of outlays is projected to remain essentially flat as a share of mandatory spending, from 39% in FY2008 to 40% in FY2018.

The CBO baseline, intended as a neutral starting point for the estimation of budgetary effects of legislative changes, is not a "best guess" of the likely future trajectory of the economy. CBO baseline projections, according to most budget experts, may tend to understate the growth of discretionary spending as a share of total federal spending, and therefore may overstate the future growth of mandatory spending.[7] CBO baseline projections assume that discretionary spending will increase at the rate of inflation over the projection period.[8] In the past, non-defense discretionary spending has grown roughly as fast as overall economic growth. If discretionary spending grew as fast as overall economic growth, rather than at the rate of inflation as in the CBO baseline projections, discretionary spending would account for 7.9% of federal spending in 2018, rather than the 6.8% in the CBO baseline projections.[9]

Continued growth of entitlement spending, especially for health care, plays a major role in the projected future imbalance between federal revenues and spending. Deficits in the next decade are projected to rise sharply due to higher health care costs and Baby Boomer retirements. The Administration and Congress will eventually need to address these fiscal imbalances. Many experts have warned of the dangers of the long-term fiscal imbalance.[10]

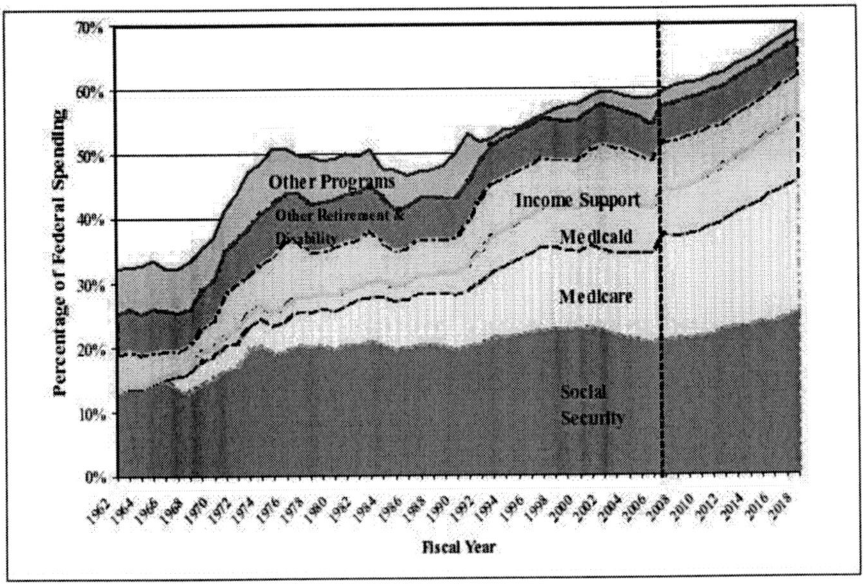

Source: CBO and OMB. CBO baseline projections depicted to the right of the vertical dotted line. Offsetting receipts are excluded.

Figure 2. Components of Mandatory Spending As a Percentage of Federal Spending

Mandatory Spending and the Economy

Calculating mandatory spending as a percentage of GDP shows what share of total economic resources are devoted to these programs. **Figure 3,** which shows the evolution of mandatory spending and its components relative to GDP since 1962, reflects the same trends that appear in **Figure 1**.

Mandatory spending, relative to the economy, grew rapidly in the late 1960s and 1970s. In the 1980s, Medicare, Medicaid, and Social Security continued to grow, while other components of mandatory spending fluctuated with the business cycle. In the 1990s, mandatory spending including offsetting receipts (about 1% of GDP) remained around 10% of the economy.

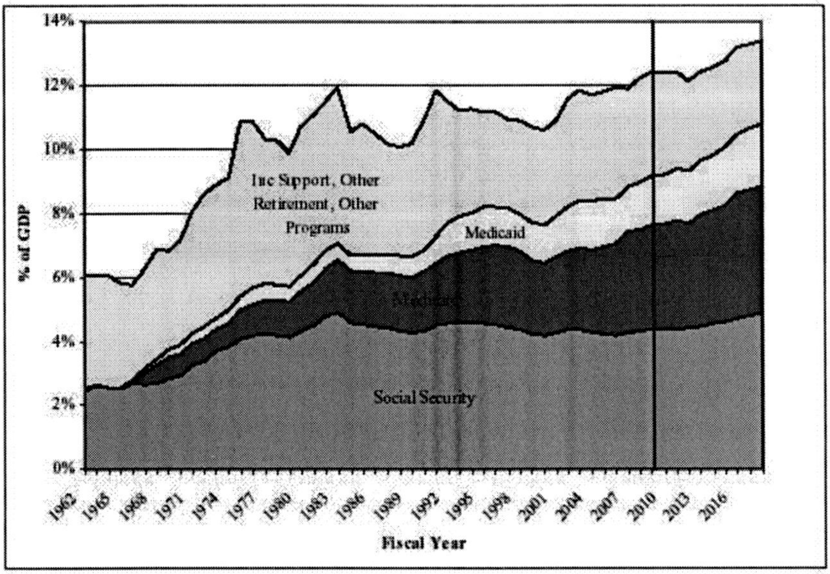

Source: CBO and OMB. CBO baseline projections depicted to the right of the vertical line. Offsetting receipts are excluded.

Figure 3. Mandatory Spending Before Offsetting Receipts As a Percentage of GDP

Social Security spending grew relative to the economy from 2.5% of GDP in 1965 to its peak of 4.9% of GDP in 1983. Since then, Social Security has fluctuated between 4.3% and 4.6% of GDP. CBO projects Social Security spending will increase from 4.6% in 2008 to 5.0% of GDP in 2018. Both Medicare and Medicaid have grown faster than the overall economy, and continued growth is expected. According to CBO current-law projections, they will total 6.0% of GDP in 2018.

During recessions, GDP falls and spending automatically increases on unemployment insurance and some means-tested programs such as Food Stamps. Spending on income support programs, therefore, has been more volatile than Social Security and Medicare spending because income support spending is more closely tied to economic fluctuations. In the 1960s, income support programs accounted for about 1% of GDP or less. In the wake of the 1974-1976 recession and the 1974 creation of the Supplemental Security Income (SSI) program, income support spending rose to over 2% of GDP. In recent years, income support spending has hovered around 1.5% of GDP and has been projected to decline gradually to 1.2% of GDP in 2018.

WHY HAS MANDATORY SPENDING RISEN?

Mandatory spending has increased in relation to total federal spending and GDP for four reasons. First, discretionary spending, defined as non-entitlement spending that is provided through appropriations acts, has fallen relative to mandatory spending. Defense expenditures once dominated domestic discretionary spending but now accounts for a relatively smaller share of federal spending. Defense discretionary expenditures as a share of GDP have trended downwards since the height of the Vietnam War in the late 1960s, despite temporary increases during the late 1970s and early 1980s. Even with recent increases in defense spending due to military action in Afghanistan and Iraq, defense spending, which accounted for 4% of GDP in 2005, took up less than half the share of the economy that it did in the late 1960s. These trends in discretionary spending are shown in **Figure 4**.

Second, domestic discretionary spending has been relatively stable as a share of GDP compared to mandatory spending, which has grown more quickly. Domestic discretionary spending, about 2.5% of GDP in the early 1960s, rose to about 4.5% of GDP in the mid-1970s, partly due to expansion of social spending and partly because of the severity of the 1974-1975 recession. In the 1980s, domestic discretionary spending as a share of GDP fell, and budget limits or "caps" helped restrict growth in discretionary spending in the 1990s. Due to slight increases in the last half dozen years, domestic discretionary spending is just over 3.5% of GDP—its approximate share for the late 1960s and early 1970s. The international component of discretionary spending, just under 1% of GDP in 1962, has declined to 0.3% of GDP in recent years.[11]

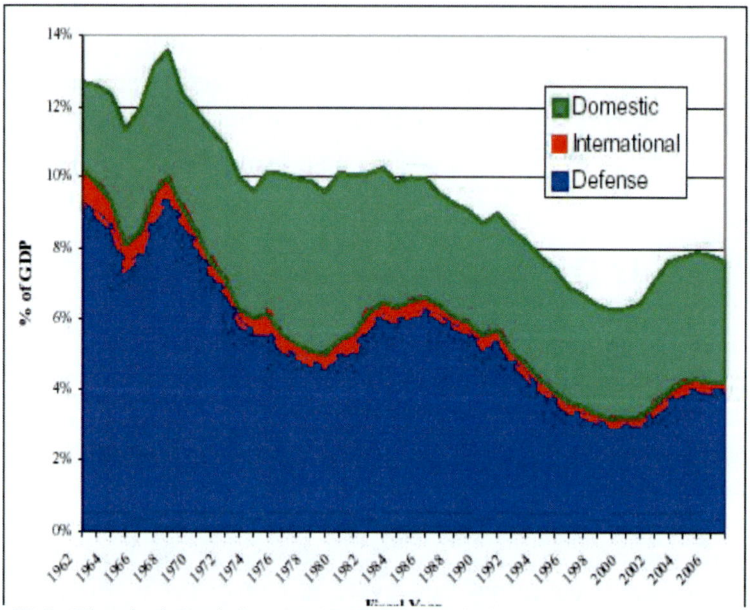

Source: CBO Historical Statistics. FY2008 data exclude supplemental funding enacted after the FY2008 Consolidated Omnibus Act (P.L. 110-161).

Figure 4. Discretionary Spending As a Percentage of GDP

Third, the number of beneficiaries of entitlement programs has grown as the average age of population has risen. The Medicare Act of 1965 extended health benefits for most retirees and greatly expanded federal financial support for indigent health care through the Medicaid program. Other programs, such as SSI and the earned income tax credit (EITC) introduced in the 1970s, also increased the number of beneficiaries. Moreover, as life expectancy has increased, the proportion of the population older than 85 has also increased, which has helped increase Social Security and Medicare spending.

Fourth, health care costs per capita have grown far faster than the overall economy. New medical technologies transformed health care in the past generation, leading to increased costs and a more intensive style of medical practice. Third-party reimbursement of health care costs by public and private insurance programs provided consumers and medical providers with few incentives to control costs until the 1980s. Health care cost growth was slowed by the introduction of Medicare's prospective payment system for hospitals in 1983 and the expanding market share of Health Maintenance Organizations (HMOs) in the mid-1980s. Attempts to control costs after the 1980s, such as the Balanced Budget Act of 1997 (P.L. 105-33), have been only temporarily or partially successful in slowing the rate of increase in health care spending.

MANDATORY SPENDING BEYOND 2018

CBO baseline projections, which extend 10 years forward, do not reflect the full force of the pressures the impending retirement of the large baby boom generation will exert on the federal budget. The oldest baby boomers reach age 65 in 2011, and most will not reach age 65 until after 2015. Extended baseline projections suggest that Social Security spending could amount to 6.4% of GDP by 2080—an increase of 2% of GDP from its 2008 level. Medicare and Medicaid spending, in large part due to rising health care costs, is projected to reach 18.5% of GDP by 2082. Long-term CBO projections using an alternative set of assumptions show Medicare and Medicaid growing to 19.3% of GDP by 2080.[12] By contrast, total federal spending in 2008 was 20.9% of GDP.

Most fiscal experts assert that avoiding the accumulation of large, unsustainable debts will require cuts in entitlement benefits, large increases in federal revenues, a significant reduction in discretionary spending, or some mix of those policies. Because federal deficits and debts have adverse economic consequences, including lower economic growth, the longer such adjustments are delayed, the more difficult those adjustments will be.

CONCLUSION

Mandatory spending has taken up an increasingly large share of federal spending over the past half century. By the end of the next decade, according to CBO baseline projections, mandatory spending will account for three out of every five dollars of federal spending. Mandatory spending has grown relative to the economy, even as the size of total federal spending relative to the overall economy has remained roughly constant.

Major entitlement programs play a larger and larger part within the category of mandatory spending. In 1962, before Medicare and Medicaid were created, Social Security accounted for just over half of all mandatory spending. Today, Social Security accounts for slightly less than 40% of mandatory spending. Medicare and Medicaid, since their inception, have taken up an increasingly large share of mandatory spending. Together those two programs' outlays now exceed Social Security spending, and CBO current-law projections indicate they could make up nearly half of mandatory spending in 2018.

Reducing the federal deficit significantly by cutting spending without reducing mandatory spending, and in particular entitlements, would be difficult. Social Security, Medicare, and Medicaid account for over three-quarters of mandatory spending and just under two-fifths of total federal outlays. Focusing budget cuts on the big three programs, however, could adversely affect the elderly or the poor. Limiting budget reductions to income support programs, such as Temporary Assistance for Needy Families (TANF), SSI, and Food Stamps, would not reduce the federal deficit by much as these programs account for about one-seventh of mandatory spending.

Most of the increases in federal spending have been occurring in Medicare and Medicaid. Furthermore, over the next 75 years, the growth in Medicare is projected to be the largest contributor to the long-term fiscal shortfall.[13] Fundamental reform of the health programs may be needed to eliminate long-term fiscal strains while preserving the goals of these programs.

APPENDIX. DISCRETIONARY SPENDING

Discretionary spending by the federal government is defined as non-entitlement spending that is provided through appropriations acts. This type of spending funds many of the activities commonly associated with federal government functions, such as running executive branch agencies, congressional offices and agencies, and international operations of the government. Essentially all spending on federal wages and salaries is discretionary.[14]

Discretionary spending is often contrasted with mandatory, or direct, spending, which the Budget Enforcement Act (BEA) of 1990 (P.L. 101-508) defines as (1) budget authority provided by law other than appropriation acts; (2) entitlement authority; and (3) the Food Stamp program. Thus, while spending for some entitlement programs, such as Medicaid and some veterans' programs, is controlled through appropriations acts, such outlays fall within the category of mandatory spending in Congressional Budget Office (CBO) summaries.[15] **Table 1** illustrates these budget categories.[16]

In FY2008, federal spending accounted for just over a fifth (20.9%) of the U.S. economy, nearly equal to its average share of gross domestic product (GDP) since FY1962. Discretionary spending accounted for 12.7% of GDP in FY1962, falling to 7.9% of GDP in FY2008. Over time, discretionary spending has fallen as a percentage of GDP due to its slower growth rate relative to the overall economy. In addition, rapid growth of entitlement outlays relative to other federal spending is another major cause of the long-term fall in discretionary spending's share of GDP.

In contrast to the longer term trends in discretionary spending, discretionary outlays over the last decade rose as a proportion of GDP from 6.3% in FY1999 to an estimated 7.9% in FY2008. This growth represents a 5% per year average increase in real terms. Defense outlays largely contributed to this increase, growing at 8% per year in real terms, while non-defense discretionary outlays grew 2.5% per year in real terms. Between FY1999 to FY2008, defense outlays grew from 3.0% to 4.3% of GDP while non-defense outlays grew from 3.0% to 3.7% of GDP.

As the recent expansion in discretionary spending illustrates, outlays in some government departments and agencies have grown very slowly or have been cut, while spending in other areas has expanded rapidly. Defense spending rose after the attacks of September 11, 2001, and the start of wars in Afghanistan and in Iraq. Funding for defense and emergency and disaster management increased sharply in the wake of hurricane Katrina, boosting overall discretionary spending further. In recent years, disaster funding has dropped sharply, allowing non-defense spending as a share of GDP to fall as well. The trajectory of future discretionary spending, especially as it relates to defense spending, depends in large part on the scale of future operations in Iraq and Afghanistan.

Discretionary spending is likely to rise over the next several fiscal years due to the current economic turmoil and resulting federal interventions to stimulate the economy. Budget estimates of federal spending and revenues for FY2009 and beyond, issued in summer 2008, were rendered largely obsolete by recent economic issues and resulting legislation enacted to reduce the impact of the housing and credit crises. New shocks to the financial system and the economy may present Congress with new demands for federal responses, which will likely affect discretionary spending levels in FY2009.

Over the longer term, projected future growth in entitlement program outlays may put severe pressure on discretionary spending unless policy changes are enacted or federal revenues are increased. Recent research on long-term fiscal challenges has focused on continued increases in the per beneficiary cost of health care, as well as the more predictable demographic changes that will occur as the Baby Boom generation retires. Projections from a variety of sources predict that spending on Medicare and Social Security will increase sharply as a share of GDP in coming decades.[17]

Table A-1. Categories of Federal Spending

	Budget Authority Provided by Law Other than Appropriation Acts	**Budget Authority Provided by Appropriation Acts**
Entitlement	—Medicare —Social Security	—Appropriated Entitlements (e.g., veter-ns' compensation, Medicaid, TANF) —Food Stamps (with caveats)
Not an Entitlement	—Mandatory non-entitlements (e.g., Forest Service payments to states)	—Discretionary Spendinga (defense, non-defense domestic discretionary, and inter-aional)

a. Discretionary spending programs. See discussion in text.

End Notes

1 Years in this chapter refer to federal fiscal years unless otherwise noted.

2 For more information on discretionary spending trends, see the Appendix.

3 For a discussion of procedural issues, see CRS Report RS20129, *Entitlements and Appropriated Entitlements in the Federal Budget Process*, by Bill Heniff Jr.

4 U.S. General Accounting Office, *Budget Issues: Inventory of Accounts With Spending Authority and Permanent Appropriations*, GAO/AIMD-96-79, May 31, 1996.

5 Officially titled "Social Security Amendments of 1965."

6 This and subsequent calculations subtract offsetting receipts from mandatory spending, and so are comparable to those in Table 1. In FY2008, offsetting receipts were 11.2% of mandatory spending before subtraction of offsetting receipts.

7 CBO baseline projections start with Congress's most recent budgetary decisions and then assume that no policy changes will be made over the projection period. For mandatory programs, the CBO baseline assumes current laws continue unchanged.

8 While some budget enforcement legislation constraining the computation of CBO baseline estimates has expired, CBO has continued to follow those legislative guidelines.

9 This calculation uses CBO's current estimate of FY2008 discretionary spending of $1,089 billion.

10 See CBO, *The Budget and Economic Outlook: An Update*, Sept. 2008, p. 22; Alan Greenspan, "Reflections on Central Banking," remarks by Chairman Alan Greenspan at a symposium sponsored by the Federal Reserve Bank of Kansas City, Jackson Hole, WY, Aug. 26, 2005; Alan J. Auerbach, William G. Gale, and Peter R. Orszag, "New Estimates of the Budget Outlook: Plus Ça Change, Plus C'est la Même Chose," *Issues in Economic Policy*, no.3, 2006; point 10 of the United States of America—2006 Article IV Consultation, Concluding Statement of the IMF Mission, May 31, 2006, available at http://www.imf.org/ external/np/ms/2006/053106.htm.

11 For more information about the trends in discretionary spending, see the Appendix.

12 CBO, *The Long-Term Budget Outlook*, Dec. 2007.

13 See CRS Report RS22232, *The Government's Long-Term Fiscal Shortfall: How Much Is Attributable to Social Security?*, by Marc Labonte.

14 Salaries for Members of Congress, the President, and federal judges as well as federal retirement and disability costs are classified as mandatory spending.

[15] For more information, see CRS Report RS20129, *Entitlements and Appropriated Entitlements in the Federal Budget Process*, by Bill Heniff Jr.

[16] The Office of Management and Budget (OMB) uses a slightly different classification of discretionary and mandatory spending.

[17] See CBO, "*The Long-Term Budget Outlook,*" December 2007; point 10 of the United States of America—2006 Article IV Consultation, Concluding Statement of the IMF Mission, May 31, 2006; and CRS Report RL33623, *Long- Term Measures of Fiscal Imbalance*, by D. Andrew Austin.

In: Federal Spending: A Riddle Wrapped ... ISBN: 978-1-60741-728-6
Editor: Frederick C. Hargis 2010 Nova Science Publishers, Inc.

Chapter 4

MANDATORY SPENDING: USING BUDGET TRIGGERS TO CONSTRAIN GROWTH

United States Government Accountability Office

WHY GAO DID THIS STUDY

Prepared as part of GAO's basic statutory responsibility for monitoring the condition of the nation's finances, the objectives of this chapter were to (1) determine the feasibility of designing and using trigger mechanisms to constrain growth in mandatory spending programs and (2) provide an analysis of the factors that led to differences between estimated and actual outlays in seven mandatory budget accounts during fiscal years 2000 through 2004.

WHAT GAO RECOMMENDS

To promote explicit scrutiny of significant growth in mandatory accounts, as mandatory spending programs are created, reexamined, or reauthorized, Congress should consider incorporating budget triggers that would signal the need for action. Further, it should determine whether in some cases it might be appropriate to consider automatically causing some action to be taken when the trigger is exceeded. Once a trigger is tripped, Congress could either accept or reject all or a portion of a proposed response to the spending growth. The Office of

Management and Budget and agencies responsible for the seven case study accounts either did not have comments or provided comments that were clarifying and/or technical in nature, which were incorporated as appropriate.

What GAO Found

One idea to constrain growth in mandatory programs is to develop program-specific triggers that, when tripped, prompt a response. A trigger could result in a "hard" or automatic response, unless Congress and the President acted to override or alter it. Alternatively, reaching a trigger could require a "soft" response, such as a report on the causes of the overage, development of a plan to address it, or an explicit and formal decision to accept or reject a proposed action or increase. By identifying significant increases in the spending path of a mandatory program relatively early and acting to constrain it, Congress may avert larger financial challenges in the future. However, both in establishing triggers and in designing the subsequent responses, the integrity of program goals needs to be preserved. In addition, tax expenditures operate like mandatory programs but do not compete in the annual appropriations process. The analysis GAO applied to spending in this chapter would also be useful in examining tax expenditures.

The budget experts GAO consulted had mixed views of triggers. Proponents of triggers noted that mandatory spending is currently unconstrained and a mechanism that causes decision makers to at least periodically reevaluate spending is better than allowing spending to rise unchecked. Others, however, expressed considerable skepticism about the effectiveness of triggers; many felt they would either be circumvented or ignored. While GAO appreciates the views expressed by budget experts, in our opinion establishing budget triggers warrants consideration in efforts to constrain significant and largely unchecked growth in mandatory programs. However, recognizing the natural tension in balancing both long-term fiscal challenges and other public policy goals, each program needs to be considered individually to ensure that any responses triggered strike the appropriate balance between the long-term fiscal challenge and the program goals.

To better understand growth in mandatory spending and thus inform GAO's thinking on triggers, for seven case study accounts GAO categorized the reasons provided by agencies for differences between estimated and actual outlays during a 5-year period as the result of legislative, economic, or technical changes. Out of 40 differences, subsequent legislation was the primary reason for 19, economic changes for 7, and technical changes for 13. In many cases, a combination of these factors caused the differences.

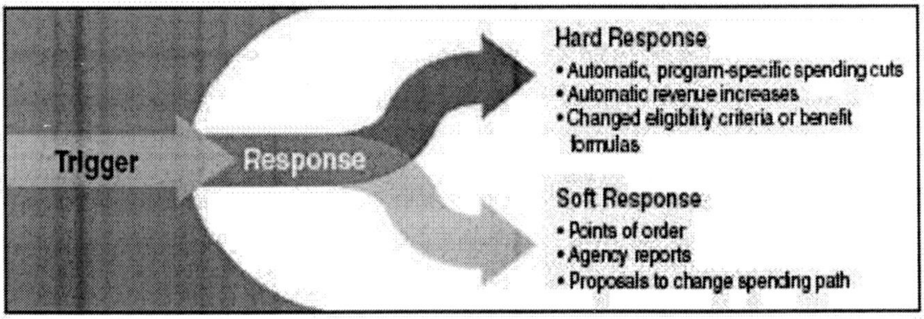

Source: GAO analysis.

Conceptual Differences between Hard and Soft Responses

ABBREVIATIONS

AMT	Alternative Minimum Tax
BBRA	Medicare, Medicaid, and SCHIP Balanced Budget
Refinement Act	
	of 1999
BEA	Budget Enforcement Act
CBO	Congressional Budget Office
CCC	Commodity Credit Corporation
CCP	Countercyclical Payments
CMS	Centers for Medicare & Medicaid Services
CRS	Congressional Research Service
ESAA	Employment Security Administration Account
EUCA	Extended Unemployment Compensation Account
FDLP	Federal Direct Student Loan Program
FFELP	Federal Family Education Loan Program
FMAP	Federal Medical Assistance Percentage
FSA	Farm Service Agency
FUA	Federal Unemployment Account
FY	Fiscal Year
GDP	Gross Domestic Product
GRH	Gramm-Rudman-Hollings Act

HI	Hospital Insurance
LDP	Loan Deficiency Payments
MMA	Medicare Prescription Drug, Improvement, and Modernization Actof 2003
MMI	Mutual Mortgage Insurance Program Account
NRRIT	National Railroad Retirement Investment Trust
OASDI	Old Age, Survivors, and Disability Insurance
OMB	Office of Management and Budget
PAYGO	Pay-As-You-Go
PPS	Prospective Payment System
QIO	Quality Improvement Organizations
RRB	Railroad Retirement Board
RUG	Resource Utilization Group
SGR	Sustainable Growth Rate
SMI	Supplementary Medical Insurance
SNF	Skilled Nursing Facility
TEUC	Temporary Extended Unemployment Compensation Act of 2002
USDA	U.S. Department of Agriculture
UTF	Unemployment Trust Fund

Over the next few decades as the baby boom generation retires and health care costs continue to rise, federal spending on retirement and health programs—Social Security, Medicare, Medicaid, and other federal pension, health, and disability programs—will grow dramatically. Absent policy changes on the spending and/or revenue sides of the budget, a growing imbalance between expected federal spending and tax revenues will mean escalating and ultimately unsustainable federal deficits and debt that threaten our future economy and national security as well as the standard of living for the American people.[1]

Given rising deficits, the expiration of the Budget Enforcement Act (BEA) of 1990,[2] and the long-term fiscal outlook, new budget control mechanisms are needed. Accordingly, there have been calls for the reintroduction of discretionary spending caps and PAYGO rules. Although PAYGO was effective in preventing legislative actions that increased the deficit, it did not address increases that occurred absent legislative action. Constraining the growth of existing mandatory spending programs requires additional action.

In our 1994 report on capping mandatory spending,[3] we noted that an alternative method to prompt congressional review of mandatory spending trends would be to require Congress to vote periodically on whether or not to make program changes when mandatory spending exceeds certain targets. One way to do this and potentially achieve greater fiscal responsibility would be to create triggers for individual mandatory programs—predetermined spending or revenue thresholds—that signal the need for some type of action to be taken on the program. Once tripped, the trigger could drive either a review or an automatic action. It could, for example, trigger a requirement for Congress to either review or reaffirm acceptance of the unexpected increase in actual program spending or projections. Alternatively, it could trigger previously specified changes to the program that automatically take effect to reduce spending or increase program revenue.

Insufficient transparency regarding both the expected and actual cost path for spending and revenue decisions hampers the ability of decision makers to make informed choices. In previous work, we have called for increased disclosure and recognition of long-term costs of proposed policies and programs.[4] The ability to monitor actual spending paths can also play an important role in decisions about both the overall fiscal position and the allocation of scarce resources. Moreover, as we reported in 1994, a cap on mandatory spending would have little if any effect on the longer-term growth trends until and unless issues of underlying program eligibility and benefits are addressed.[5] Thus, efforts to constrain growth in mandatory programs need to be focused on and tailored to individual programs. One way to assess mandatory spending is to analyze growth by examining the estimated and actual outlays for each program. Because budget estimates can be linked to achieving fiscal responsibility in the government, identifying and understanding recurring patterns between mandatory account budget estimates and actual results can facilitate future budget decisions.

This chapter, prepared as part of our basic statutory responsibility for monitoring the condition of the nation's finances, examines issues related to using such triggers on mandatory programs. The objectives were to (1) determine the feasibility of designing and using trigger mechanisms to constrain growth in mandatory spending and (2) provide an analysis of the factors that led to differences between estimated and actual outlays in seven mandatory budget accounts during fiscal years 2000 through 2004.

This chapter does not deal with the question of projected costs at the time decisions are made but instead with the need for responses when there is significant growth. Analogous analyses could be applied to the revenue side of the budget (e.g., tax expenditures).

RESULTS IN BRIEF

One idea to constrain growth in mandatory programs is to develop triggers that, when tripped, prompt a response. A trigger could result in a "hard" or automatic response, unless Congress and the President acted to override or alter it. Alternatively, reaching a trigger could require a "soft" response, such as a report on the causes of the overage, development of a plan to address it, or an explicit and formal decision to accept or reject a proposed action or increase. By identifying significant increases in the spending path of a mandatory program relatively early and acting to constrain it, Congress may avert larger financial challenges in the future. However, both in establishing triggers and in designing the subsequent actions to be triggered, the integrity of program goals needs to be preserved.

The budget experts we consulted had mixed views of triggers. Some expressed strong support for budget triggers. These proponents of triggers noted that mandatory spending is currently unconstrained and a mechanism that causes decision makers to at least periodically reevaluate spending is better than allowing spending to rise unchecked. Others, however, expressed considerable skepticism about the effectiveness of triggers; many felt they would be circumvented or ignored. For example, one expert pointed to "accounting tricks" that have resulted from triggers with hard responses, such as when Congress mandated certain costs not be counted against spending limits so as to avoid across-the-board cuts. Others worried that applying budget triggers to various mandatory programs diverts attention from what they see as the real source of the nation's fiscal woes—health care spending. Further, they felt that establishing triggers on such programs could mislead the public into thinking that the long-term fiscal problem had been addressed, thus delaying efforts to appropriately address it.

Any discussion to create triggered responses and their design must recognize that unlike controls on discretionary spending, there is some tension between the idea of triggers and the nature of entitlement and other mandatory spending programs. These programs—as with tax provisions such as tax expenditures—were designed to provide benefits based on eligibility formulas or actions as opposed to an annual decision regarding spending. This tension makes it more challenging to constrain costs and to design both triggers and triggered responses. At the same time, with only about one-third of the budget under the control of the annual appropriations process, considering ways to increase transparency, oversight, and control of mandatory programs must be part of addressing the nation's long-term fiscal challenges.

Ignoring significant growth in mandatory accounts is inconsistent with evaluation of programs and their costs. While we appreciate the concerns raised by budget experts, we believe that, if carefully designed, budget constraint mechanisms such as triggers should be considered as existing programs are reexamined or reauthorized and when new programs are created. Each program would need to be considered individually to ensure that any actions that are triggered preserve program goals. The seven mandatory accounts we examined helped inform our thinking about budget constraint mechanisms, and we present illustrative examples of how growth could be constrained in many of the accounts discussed in appendix I.

For seven case study accounts,[6] we categorized the reasons provided by agencies for differences between estimated and actual outlays during fiscal years 2000 through 2004 as the result of (1) legislative changes enacted after original estimates were submitted, (2) economic changes such as interest and unemployment rates, or (3) technical changes, which is a residual category that represents revisions to budget estimates that cannot be attributed to legislative or economic factors. Our analysis of the reasons for differences between estimated and actual outlays showed that out of 40 differences, legislative changes[7] were the primary reason for 19, economic changes for 7, and technical changes for 13. In one case, it was unclear which factors most significantly caused the difference between estimated and actual outlays. In many cases, a combination of factors caused the differences.

OMB and agencies responsible for the seven case study accounts either did not have comments or provided comments that were clarifying and/or technical in nature. These comments were incorporated as appropriate.

BACKGROUND

BEA[8] divided federal spending into two broad categories: discretionary and mandatory. Discretionary spending refers to outlays from budget authority that is provided in and controlled by appropriation acts; it can and has been controlled through annual, adjustable dollar limits (spending caps) that permanently lower the base for future appropriations. Mandatory spending[9] refers to outlays resulting from budget authority that is provided in laws other than appropriation acts, for example, entitlement programs such as Medicare, Food Stamps, and veterans' pensions. Mandatory spending—like tax expenditures—is governed by eligibility rules and benefit formulas, which means that funds are spent as required to provide benefits to those who are eligible and wish to participate. Therefore, unforeseen events such as changes in the economy or additional demands for services can translate into unanticipated additional program outlays. Congress controls spending for these programs indirectly by defining eligibility and setting the benefit or payment rules rather than directly through appropriation acts. On an annual basis, however, mandatory spending is relatively uncontrollable since Congress and the President must change substantive law in order to further increase or decrease outlays. This makes it more challenging to constrain costs and to design both triggers and triggered responses.

Over the past 4 decades, we have seen mandatory spending grow as a share of the total federal budget. For example, figure 1 shows that spending on mandatory programs rose from approximately 42 percent of total federal spending in 1984 to about 49 percent in 1994, and to 54 percent in 2004. This growth is projected to continue with mandatory programs claiming about 58 percent of total federal spending in 2010.

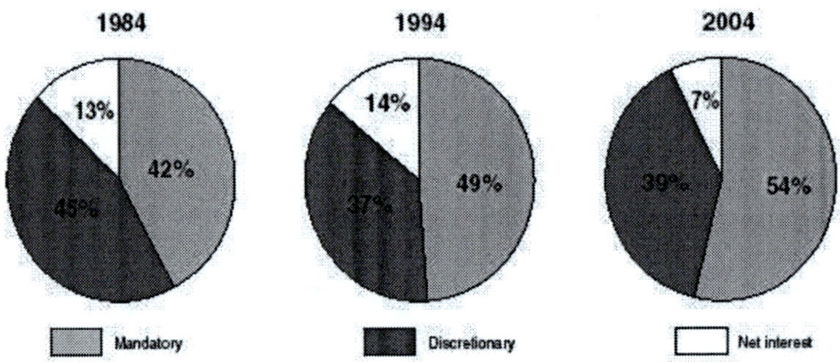

Source: GAO analysis of President's budget data.

Figure 1. Federal Spending for Mandatory and Discretionary Programs

The nation's long-term fiscal outlook is daunting under many different policy scenarios and assumptions. For instance, under a fiscally restrained scenario, if discretionary spending grew only with inflation over the next 10 years and all existing tax cuts expire when scheduled under current law, spending for Social Security and health care programs would grow to consume over three-quarters of federal revenues by 2040 (see figure 2). On the other hand, if discretionary spending grew at the same rate as the economy—measured by Gross Domestic Product (GDP)—in the near term and if all tax cuts were extended, federal revenues may just be adequate to pay interest on the growing federal debt by 2040 (see figure. 3). Numerous alternative scenarios can be developed incorporating different combinations of possible policy choices and economic assumptions, but these two scenarios can be viewed as "bookends" showing a range of possible outcomes.

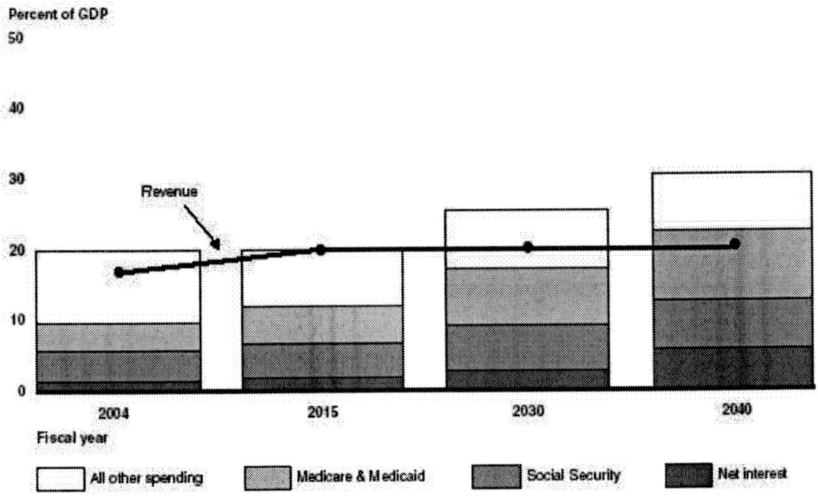

Source: GAO's August 2005 analysis.

Note: In addition to the expiration of tax cuts, revenue as a share of GDP increases through 2015 due to (1) real bracket creep, (2) more taxpayers becoming subject to the alternative minimum tax (AMT), and (3) increased revenue from tax-deferred retirement accounts. After 2015, revenue as a share of GDP is held constant.

Figure 2. Composition of Spending as a Share of GDP under Baseline Extended

As both these simulations illustrate, absent policy changes on the spending and/or revenue side of the budget, the growth in spending on federal retirement and health entitlements will encumber an escalating share of the government's resources. Neither slowing the growth in discretionary spending nor allowing the tax provisions to expire—nor both together—would eliminate the imbalance. Although revenues will be part of the debate about our fiscal future, making no changes to Social Security, Medicare, Medicaid, and other drivers of the long-term fiscal gap would require at least a doubling of taxes—and that seems implausible. Accordingly, substantive reform of Social Security and our major health programs remains critical to recapturing our future fiscal flexibility.

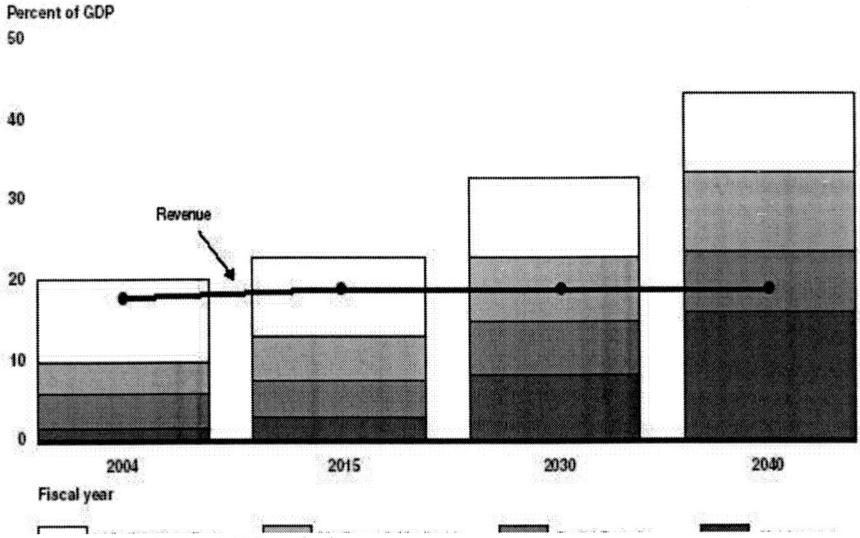

Source: GAO's August 2005 analysis.

Note: Although expiring tax provisions are extended, revenue as a share of GDP increases through 2015 due to (1) real bracket creep, (2) more taxpayers becoming subject to the AMT, and (3) increased revenue from tax-deferred retirement accounts. After 2015, revenue as a share of GDP is held constant.

Figure 3. Composition of Spending as a Share of GDP Assuming Discretionary Spending Grows with GDP After 2005 and All Expiring Tax Provisions Are Extended

These long-term spending projections can largely be attributed to the aging population and increased health care costs. This does not, however, mean that the rest of the budget should be exempt from review. It is important to periodically look at mandatory accounts in order to determine possible ways to constrain spending and ensure a more accurate and responsible federal budget process.

Congressional interest in fiscal discipline and the adoption of budget tools to control mandatory spending are not new. The Balanced Budget and Emergency Deficit Control Act of 1985, commonly referred to as Gramm-Rudman-Hollings (GRH), established declining deficit targets and a sequestration procedure to reduce spending if those targets were exceeded. GRH was amended several times, most significantly by BEA in 1990. One important reason for BEA's success in reducing the deficit during the 1990s was that the process enforced a previously reached agreement to reduce the deficit. However, recurring surpluses at the end of the decade caused a new debate to emerge and undermined the acceptance of

BEA's spending caps and PAYGO enforcement. BEA rules were not extended beyond their scheduled expiration date at the end of fiscal year 2002.

In the past, mandatory spending caps were proposed as a way to control the growth of mandatory programs. This idea was discussed in a report we issued in 1994.[10] Mandatory caps fail to address underlying eligibility and benefits formulas—which drive spending. In addition, if caps were imposed in the context of a control requiring across-the-board spending cuts, they would present agencies with difficulties in successfully reducing their program spending to stay within limits, and perhaps lead to a cycle of continual sequestrations. This difficulty is because in such a regime, any shortfalls in savings or growth in spending that occurred despite agency efforts would be added to the amount of cuts required in the next year. Moreover, the mandatory programs that would be most affected by a cap—because of their high and/or volatile growth rates—are also the programs for which a cap would be hardest to implement.

In the mid-1990s, there was a period when the idea of constraining greater-than-expected growth through the use of triggers surfaced. However, it coincided with a period when actual growth generally was less than expected. Recently, with the reappearance of large deficits, there has been a resurgence of interest in restoring budget controls and containing the growth in both discretionary and mandatory spending. For example, in 2005, numerous bills to reinstate fiscal discipline were proposed.[11] Moreover, in May 2005, OMB issued a memo to agencies that required them to propose offsets to any administrative action that would increase mandatory spending.

Budget estimates and actual outlays are determined over a period that spans nearly 2 years: from the time the President's budget is formulated, about a year before the start of the fiscal year in question, to the completion of that fiscal year. Within this 2-year lag period between original estimates and actual outlays, legislative, economic, and technical factors can affect program outlays. Budget estimates are revised part way through the fiscal year and included in the budget request for the following fiscal year. These revisions reflect updated technical and economic assumptions as well as any legislative changes. Also, midsession reviews conducted during the summer, usually in July, update budget estimates prior to the completion of the fiscal year. In addition, both CBO and OMB estimate the cost of bills that affect mandatory spending.

OBJECTIVES, SCOPE, AND METHODOLOGY

The objectives of this study were to (1) determine the feasibility of designing and using trigger mechanisms to constrain growth in mandatory spending and (2) provide an analysis of the factors (legislative, economic, and technical) that led to differences between estimated and actual outlays in seven mandatory budget accounts during fiscal years 2000 through 2004. This second objective contributed to our understanding of programs, helped us better appreciate the reasons behind growth in mandatory accounts that experienced relatively large dollar changes, and more fully informed our thinking about triggers.

To accomplish our first objective, we performed a literature search on mechanisms to constrain mandatory spending and had discussions with numerous budget experts from OMB, CBO, the Senate Budget Committee staff, and various policy research organizations. Based on our research, interviews at agencies, and discussions with experts, we then considered possible approaches for budgetary constraint within each account.

To accomplish our second objective we extracted from OMB's budget database mandatory outlays of accounts where 50 percent or more of the outlays were mandatory. We analyzed these data for fiscal years 2000 through 2004. To determine the estimated and actual outlays for each year, we used the original budget estimate and the actual outlays reported 2 years later, after the end of the fiscal year. For example, when determining the difference between estimated and actual outlays for fiscal year 2000, we compared the fiscal year 2000 budget estimates published in February 1999 to the actual outlays published in February 2001.

From the 534 accounts with outlays at least half mandatory, we selected the top 10 accounts that experienced the greatest average dollar change between original estimate and actual outlays in absolute value terms for 5 fiscal years (2000–2004). The complete list of these accounts is included as appendix III. These 10 accounts, which represent approximately 50 percent of total average mandatory outlays, include (1) Interest on Treasury Debt Securities, (2) Unemployment Trust Fund, (3) Commodity Credit Corporation Fund,[12] (4) Federal Supplementary Medical Insurance Trust Fund (Medicare Part B), (5) Federal Hospital Insurance Trust Fund (Medicare Part A), (6) Grants to States for Medicaid,[13] (7) Rail Industry Pension Fund, (8) Federal Direct Student Loan Program (FDLP) Account, (9) Payments to Health Care Trust Funds, and (10) Mutual Mortgage Insurance Program Account (MMI). Because many of the programs we selected are relatively big, large dollar increases may represent small percentage increases relative to program size.

After initial analysis, we excluded three of these accounts from further analysis: Interest on Treasury Debt Securities, MMI,[14] and Payments to Health Care Trust Funds. We eliminated the U.S. Treasury account because interest payments are a function of all other funding decisions and thus provide little insight into trigger design.[15] We excluded the MMI account because the program itself is discretionary—only the large mandatory reestimates of its credit subsidy required by the Federal Credit Reform Act of 1990 caused it to fall into our original sample. Because decisions about the size of this program are annually made in the appropriations process and can be informed by the reestimates of previous years' loans, there is no need for separate triggers. Finally, we excluded the Payments to Health Care Trust Funds account because the payments are classified as intragovernmental transfers and therefore do not affect overall budget outlay data. Moreover, these transfers are captured within other accounts in our sample.

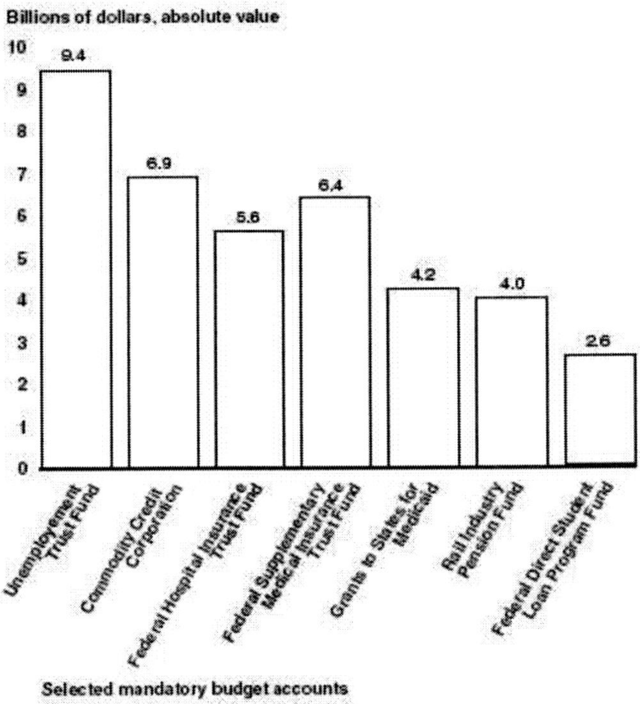

Source: GAO analysis of President's budget data.

Figure 4. Five-Year Average Differences between Estimated and Actual Mandatory Outlays, Fiscal Years 2000 through 2005

Figure 4 above shows the 5-year average difference between estimated and actual mandatory outlays in absolute value terms for the seven accounts we reviewed. These differences ranged from $9.4 billion in the Unemployment Trust Fund to $2.6 billion in FDLP.

To gain more perspective on what factors contributed to the differences between estimated and actual outlays in the remaining seven accounts, we met with officials from the cognizant agencies to determine if the reasons behind the differences were (1) legislative, (2) economic, (3) technical, or a combination of the three. We did not independently verify the explanations agencies provided for differences.

Our work was done between May 2005 and January 2006 in Washington, D.C., in accordance with generally accepted government auditing standards.

TRIGGER MECHANISMS COULD HELP CONSTRAIN MANDATORY SPENDING BUT MUST BE CAREFULLY DESIGNED

The purpose of a budget trigger is to either automatically cause some action to occur or to prompt decision makers to evaluate and consider responding to rising costs. For example, where differences between expected and actual growth in a program exceed a specified amount, Congress could decide explicitly—by voting—whether to accept the slippage or could take action to bring the spending path closer to the original goal by recouping some or all of the slippage through changes in the program. Our background research, work in case study agencies, and discussions with budget experts highlighted several issues to consider when designing triggers and their resulting actions, such as the extent of agreement among decision makers about underlying fiscal goals, measures selected to trip the trigger, and the triggered response.

While a budget process can surface important issues, it is not a substitute for substantive debate—no process can force agreement where one does not exist. Accordingly, the success of any effort to constrain growth depends on whether there is widespread agreement on the underlying goals; absent such agreement, any trigger would likely be circumvented. For example, underlying the successful budget enforcement mechanisms embodied in BEA was the broadly accepted goal of deficit reduction and an agreement on a specific set of legislative changes to reach that goal. Its triggers were centered around measures that Congress could control—discretionary spending caps and changes to entitlement and tax laws.

However, once the budget moved into surplus in the late 1990s and there was no longer agreement on fiscal goals, actions were taken to bypass BEA controls. For example, the consolidated appropriations acts for both fiscal years 2000 and 2001 mandated that OMB change the PAYGO scorecard balance to zero. Both OMB and CBO estimated that without instructions to change the scorecard, sequestrations would have been required in 2001.

Other countries we have studied have sought to address national priorities by developing explicit goals to guide fiscal policy and justifying their goals with compelling rationales that often pointed out the potential fiscal and economic benefits of budgetary discipline. In a 2000 report,[16] we noted that having fiscal goals anchored by a rationale that is compelling enough to make continued restraint acceptable is critical to sustain support for budgetary discipline.

Issues to Consider in Constructing a Trigger

One of the reasons for the success of BEA was its link to congressional action.[17] Discretionary spending caps and PAYGO constrained congressional action—BEA held Congress accountable only for things it could control and not for the effect of economic or technical factors on spending or revenues. This was both the strength and the limitation of PAYGO. Triggers seek to go beyond the PAYGO regime by subjecting program growth to scrutiny even where that growth is the result of economic, population, or other factors outside congressional control. Triggers recognize that even the best estimates can turn out to be wrong and that decision makers who expected one path might wish to consider changes in a program where the path is significantly different from what was anticipated.

In general, there are two types of responses to budget triggers—soft and hard—depending on what type of action results when the trigger is tripped. A "soft" response prompts special consideration of a program or a proposal for action when a certain threshold or target is breached. Examples of soft responses that could be triggered include requiring the administering agency to prepare a special report explaining why the trigger's threshold was breached, or requiring the President to submit a proposal for reform. An example of a soft response already exists in the Medicare program, which requires the President to submit a proposal to Congress for action if the Medicare Trustees determine in 2 consecutive years that the general revenue share of Medicare spending is projected to exceed 45 percent during a 7-year period.[18] In addition, a few Social Security reform proposals have included language requiring presidential and congressional action if the Social Security Board of Trustees determines that the balance ratio of either of the Social Security trust funds will be zero for any calendar year during the succeeding 75 years.[19]

Soft responses can help in alerting decision makers of potential problems but they do not ensure that action to decrease spending or increase revenue is taken. With soft responses, the fiscal path continues unless Congress and the President take action. In contrast, a trigger could lead to “hard” responses requiring a predetermined, program-specific action to take place, such as changes in eligibility criteria and benefit formulas, automatic revenue increases, or automatic spending cuts. With hard responses, spending is automatically constrained, revenue is automatically increased, or both, unless Congress takes action to override. Figure 5 below illustrates the conceptual differences between hard and soft responses of a budget trigger.

In establishing triggers, both near- and long-term perspectives need be considered. For some programs it might be appropriate to tie triggers to historical data. For example, unexpected spending growth in student loans might be measured against past historical spending data. However, for other programs that expose the government to long-term commitments—such as Medicare or Social Security—it might be more appropriate to tie the trigger to projections of future spending. Social Security, however, represents a large long-term commitment of future resources. Thus, growth for this program might be measured against changes in actuarial projections of Social Security’s 75-year outlook. Such an approach could be used for other programs with long-term commitments, such as pension insurance, if good long-term projections become available.

Since all estimates are subject to some uncertainty, the triggering mechanism should not be so tight that it is overly sensitive to normal variation in budget estimation. One way to address this concern is to establish a normal or expected range of budget uncertainty and set a trigger level that falls outside this range. For example, if a program’s actual outlays historically fall within plus or minus 5 percent of estimated outlays, a trigger set at a level greater than 5 percent would best signal unexpected growth. This approach resembles one CBO uses for certain programs to analyze the budgetary effects of legislative proposals.[20] Using a probabilistic model, CBO estimates the weighted average of the effects associated with all possible sets of circumstances, taking into account their respective probabilities. Such an approach could be adapted to establish a range of uncertainty around a budget estimate.

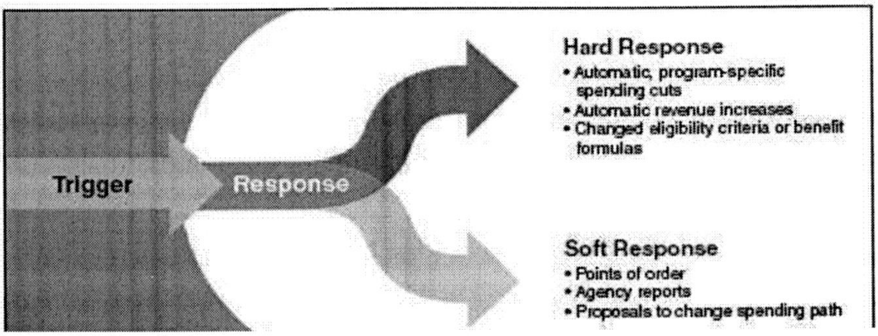

Source: GAO analysis.

Figure 5. Conceptual Differences between Hard and Soft Responses

Triggers also could be used to ensure that policy changes actually achieve intended reductions in spending growth. Such triggers could address concerns that some budget constraint mechanisms create the false impression that long-term problems have been addressed.

Although any hard response can be overridden by congressional action, it could be important to incorporate a more automatic escape clause into budget enforcement mechanisms such as triggers. Effective budget enforcement mechanisms need to be able to accommodate changing budget policy and political environments in which future outcomes are difficult to predict. For example, periods of economic growth may be brief or sustained, but inevitably are followed by periods of economic downturn that may be shallow or deep. Escape mechanisms, such as expiration dates, allow budget policies and procedures to be renegotiated later. In addition to expiration dates, House or Senate rules can provide flexibility. For example, any Senator may raise a point of order against legislation violating PAYGO rules prohibiting consideration of revenue or direct spending legislation that is not deficit-neutral. However, the point of order may be waived if there is broad consensus on the need to do so—that is, if there is an affirmative vote of three-fifths of the membership.

Although they provide important flexibility, escape clauses can be overused. For example, in fiscal year 2002, the Department of Defense and Emergency Supplemental Appropriations Act[21] instructed that $130.3 billion in costs be eliminated from the PAYGO scorecard. Both OMB and CBO estimated that without instructions to change the scorecard, a sequester—across-the-board spending cuts—would have been required in 2002. In addition, many programs were exempt from PAYGO's sequestration requirement. These exemptions meant that the full brunt of any sequester was concentrated in the remaining programs, resulting in cuts so draconian that Congress and the President changed the targets rather than impose the required cuts.

Issues to Consider in Designing the Triggered Response

Whether a triggered response is soft, hard, or a combination of the two, efforts to constrain growth in mandatory programs need to be focused at the program level. The experience with GRH highlights the importance of individually designed triggers and responses. The deficit-neutrality targets under GRH triggered a hard response—across-the-board spending cuts—if they were not met. The deficit targets under GRH were not achieved due to the inability of Congress and the President to control all of the factors—mainly economic factors—that affected whether the trigger would be breached and their unwillingness to accept the across-the-board cuts that would have been necessary to meet the deficit targets.

In developing program-specific triggers and responses, proposed changes in underlying benefits structure and design of mandatory programs can be considered in the context of the factors that drove the growth and the goals and objectives of specific programs. For example, certain programs such as unemployment insurance and crop assistance are designed and intended to have a countercyclical effect on the economy. That is, they are aimed at reducing the size and duration of swings in economic activity in order to keep economic growth closer to a pace consistent with low inflation and high employment. Thus, a triggered response in these programs needs to be sensitive to whether growth is being driven by automatic budget stabilizers. For example, a rise in the unemployment rate would by design increase outlays in federal unemployment insurance not only to provide assistance to the unemployed but also to stabilize the economy. If a trigger were established that resulted in a contractionary response, it could undermine these important goals and exacerbate the effects of unemployment on the economy. In a January 2002 report,[22] the Congressional Research Service (CRS) suggested one option to avoid procyclical triggers would be to delegate to some entity—for instance Congress or an executive department—the responsibility for evaluating each year whether deteriorating economic conditions would make a trigger detrimental. If conditions were found to be deteriorating, decisions would need to be made about whether and how to implement any reduction. CRS acknowledged, however, that this type of proposal could be criticized on the grounds that it is based on a subjective decision and thus could be prey to the sort of political pressures that critics fear would undermine a trigger. Indeed, one budget expert we met with expressed concern that in devising a budget trigger, it would be helpful to acknowledge political pressures by considering who would judge progress against the trigger and the neutrality of the judging entity.

The programs and agencies we reviewed have objectives and missions that contribute to the achievement of public policy goals such as income security, feeding the nation, fostering higher education, and providing health care. To these ends, these programs are designed to provide entitlements—benefits and assistance—to eligible recipients. While striving to meet these commitments, our nation is faced with a daunting long-term fiscal outlook based on the challenges of an aging population, unsustainable deficits, and mounting debt while also ensuring truth and transparency. Figure 6 depicts the inherent tension in balancing public policy goals and long-term fiscal challenges.

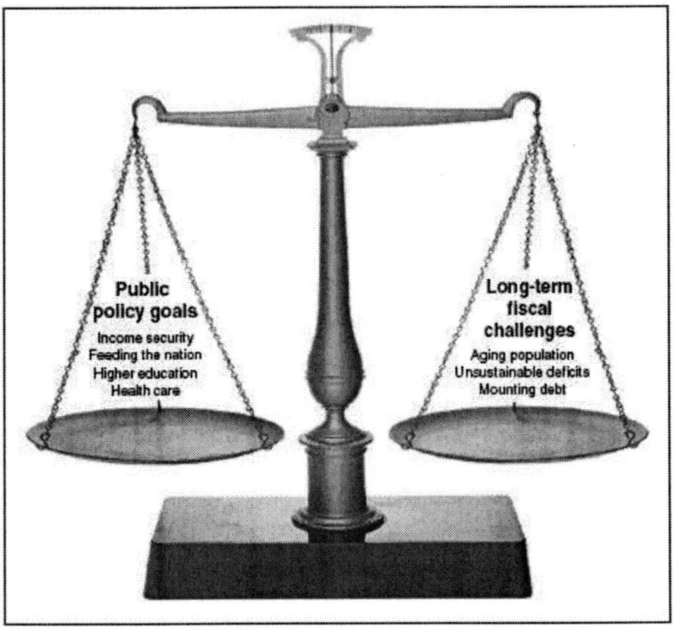

Source: GAO analysis and PhotoDisc (images).

Figure 6. Balancing Public Policy Goals and Long-term Fiscal Challenges

Addressing this tension invariably entails difficult political choices among competing programs that promise benefits to many Americans but are collectively unaffordable and unsustainable at current revenue levels. In February 2005 we highlighted the size of fiscal imbalances looming in the future and the challenge of our policy process to act with more foresight to take early action on problems that may not constitute an urgent crisis but pose important longer-term threats to the nation's fiscal, economic, security, and societal future.[23] Budget triggers are mechanisms that can encourage and facilitate such action.

To help us better consider the implications of establishing triggers, we looked at seven mandatory accounts with relatively large differences between estimated and actual outlays: Commodity Credit Corporation (CCC), Federal Direct Student Loan Program Account, Grants to States for Medicaid, Federal Hospital Insurance (HI) Trust Fund (Medicare Part A), Federal Supplementary Medical Insurance (SMI) Trust Fund (Medicare Part B), Rail Industry Pension Fund, and the Unemployment Trust Fund. We explored ways in which existing triggers and their corresponding actions could be revised, as well as an array of new trigger mechanisms that take into consideration the issues just discussed and could be adopted to promote better budgeting in light of the nation's long-term fiscal outlook.

It is important to consider the data upon which the trigger will hinge—future projections based on historical data, growth as a percent of GDP, total growth, or another measure altogether. For example, Congress has established a trigger to constrain growth in Medicare spending for physicians' services. The sustainable growth rate (SGR) is a statutorily set formula that estimates the allowed rate of increase in spending for physicians' services; that rate is used to construct the spending target for the following calendar year. If actual spending exceeds the cumulative SGR targets, fee updates in future years must be lowered sufficiently both to offset the accumulated excess spending and to slow expected spending for the coming year.[24] The Medicare Prescription Drug, Improvement, and Modernization Act of 2003 (MMA) established another trigger—the general revenue share of Medicare spending. If the Medicare Trustees determine in 2 consecutive years that the general revenue share is projected to exceed 45 percent during a 7-year projection period, the President must submit a proposal to Congress for action. To date, this threshold has not been breached and thus no response has been triggered. However, Medicare Trustees are expected to determine the first breach in their upcoming 2006 report as the trigger is projected to be tripped in 2012, which falls within the 7-year projection period captured in that report. For unemployment insurance, a trigger was established around balances in the Unemployment Trust Fund. When funds accumulating in federal unemployment accounts reach statutorily set limits, a distribution of the "excess" funds from the trust fund to individual states' accounts—called "Reed

Distributions"[25]—are automatically triggered based on each state's share of covered wages. One way to constrain federal spending would be to increase the statutory cap on federal unemployment accounts, thus making it more difficult to trigger Reed Distributions to states. By making it more difficult to trip the trigger, funds could continue to build during economic prosperity and be available to states when truly needed to counter rising unemployment.

Our analysis allowed us to develop a list of illustrative examples, which analyze the related trade-offs involved in balancing restraint with optimization of program goals. These are shown in appendix I, along with a brief description of the program and account. Finally, where appropriate we present illustrative examples of hard responses that could be established to constrain spending. We do not specifically advocate any of these approaches—they are presented for illustrative purposes only to provide a sense of the types of trigger and resulting actions that could be established. Although the illustrative examples we developed apply specifically to the seven case study accounts that we reviewed, we believe the information can further the larger policy conversation about how to increase oversight of the path of mandatory spending and advance and encourage budgetary discipline.

Expert Views on Trigger Mechanisms Are Mixed

We interviewed budget experts from OMB, CBO, the Senate Budget Committee staff, and various policy research organizations to discuss views on using triggers to constrain mandatory spending. Overall, views were mixed. While some were more in favor of triggers than others, many expressed concern that they would be circumvented or ignored, thereby questioning their effectiveness. In addition, many were concerned that triggers could jeopardize the underlying intent of mandatory programs. Several experts also pointed to the need to ensure that any triggers developed be carefully designed to avoid procyclical effects.

Some of the experts expressed strong support for budget triggers. These individuals believed that triggers with hard responses had the potential to constrain mandatory spending and that the accountability added by triggers would be preferable to the current unconstrained environment.

For example, one expressed concern about the debt burden being permitted to mount for future generations in order to avoid the reduction in benefits or increase in taxes needed to finance current benefits. Linking revenues and spending with GDP, she argued, would help avoid such generational inequities. Another added that under current policy, spending grows automatically, by default, faster than tax revenues as the population ages and health costs soar. He argued that only by changing the budget's autopilot programming can we gain the flexibility needed to continually improve government policies and services.

Others, however, said that triggers reduced accountability because they enable decision makers to publicly extol budget constraint but quietly continue to increase spending. One pointed to "accounting tricks" that have resulted from triggers with hard responses, such as when Congress mandated certain costs not be counted against spending limits so as to avoid across-the-board cuts. However, as discussed previously, triggers also could be used to ensure that policy changes actually achieve intended reductions in spending growth. Such triggers could address concerns that some budget constraint mechanisms create the false impression that long-term problems have been addressed.

Many expressed skepticism that budget constraint mechanisms such as triggers would be adhered to; one cited Medicare's SGR as an example. The SGR system is designed to apply financial brakes whenever actual spending for physicians' services exceeds predefined spending targets. It does this by reducing physician fees or limiting their annual increase. Because the actual versus target spending comparison is cumulative, future fee updates are reduced to lower future actual spending below future target spending until total cumulative actual spending is the same as total cumulative target spending. However, fee declines were averted for 2003, 2004, and 2005 by administrative and legislative actions that modified or overrode the SGR system.

Some experts worried that applying budget triggers to various mandatory spending programs would divert attention from the real source of the nation's fiscal woes—health care—whose costs continue to rise faster than GDP. They pointed to CBO data as evidence that, outside of health care and to a lesser extent Social Security, virtually all other mandatory programs are decreasing or holding steady as a percent of GDP. Accordingly, they expressed concern that establishing triggers on such programs could mislead the public into thinking that the long-term fiscal problem had been addressed, thus delaying efforts to appropriately address it.

Many of the budget experts raised concerns about triggers jeopardizing the important underlying missions and program goals financed by mandatory accounts. In particular, concerns were raised about undermining countercyclical effects of programs such as unemployment insurance, Food Stamps, and the Earned Income Tax Credit. Some noted that the desire to preserve program goals is the reason why triggers with hard responses have not worked in the past. With respect to the SGR, for example, one expert explained that the reason Congress overrides the trigger is to ensure doctors do not stop accepting Medicare patients.

Finally, a couple of experts pointed out that triggers need not only apply to spending; the revenue side of the budget should also be addressed. One noted, for example, that an increase in taxes to cover spending growth would increase visibility to the public and thus permit the American people to be more aware of how much they are paying for services. Applying triggers to tax cuts was an issue considered in 2001 when the budget was in surplus and tax cuts were proposed. For example, Federal Reserve Chairman Greenspan at that time expressed his preference for a trigger that would make tax cuts contingent on the realized net debt level. Comptroller General Walker also raised the possibility of using a trigger to return a "surplus dividend" if actual surpluses occurred in excess of specific levels. Ultimately, however, triggers were not adopted. Instead, tax cuts were enacted through 2010 even though substantial deficits have reappeared. In addition, as we reported in a February 2005 testimony,[26] there has been an extensive use of tax incentives, rather than direct spending authority, to fund social objectives. As we reported in September 2005,[27] the sum of revenue loss estimates associated with tax expenditures—such as tax exclusions, credits, and deductions—was nearly $730 billion in 2004.[28] Many tax expenditures operate like mandatory spending programs and generally are not subject to reauthorization. Such tax expenditures are embedded in the tax system and are off the radar screen for the most part. This is a concern from a budgetary standpoint because federal dollars committed to fund these expenditures do not compete in the annual appropriations process and are effectively "fully funded" before any discretionary spending is considered. The analysis we applied to spending in this chapter would also be useful in examining tax expenditures. However, challenges in defining and measuring tax expenditures, to some extent, would affect any effort to curtail revenues foregone through tax expenditures. For example, after taxpayers have taken advantage of tax expenditures, the federal government still may not know, with much certainty, how much tax revenue was foregone, who benefited, and what results were achieved.[29]

Reasons for Differences between Estimated and Actual Outlays in Selected Accounts Varied

To better appreciate the reasons behind growth in mandatory accounts and thus inform our thinking on triggers, we examined the reasons for differences between originally estimated and actual outlays for seven mandatory accounts that experienced relatively large dollar changes.[30] Based on agencies' explanations of differences between estimated and actual outlays of the case study accounts we examined, we found that legislation enacted after original estimates were submitted was the primary driver in 19 out of 40 differences during fiscal years 2000 through 2004. Economic factors, such as changes in interest and unemployment rates, were primarily responsible for 7 differences. Finally, technical factors, which cover a broad spectrum, most significantly drove 13 out of 40 differences. In one case, it was unclear which factors most significantly caused the difference between estimated and actual outlays. In many cases, a combination of factors resulted in differences.

In categorizing agencies' explanations for differences between estimated and actual outlays, we applied criteria similar to those that CBO uses in its annual budget and economic outlook reports to categorize changes as legislative, technical, and economic. However, in our report, legislative action was classified in a somewhat different manner from the method that CBO applies. Whereas we examined the actual budgetary effect that resulted from the legislation, CBO projects the anticipated future budgetary effect of legislation.[31] Figure 7 describes the criteria that we applied to categorize agencies' explanations into three factors. While this framework is helpful in evaluating changes in the federal budget, it is not precise and should be viewed as indicative as opposed to determinative.

- *Legislative*: Refers to any legislative action that (1) was enacted *after* the time that original budget estimates were submitted in a given fiscal year and (2) proved to have a direct effect on account outlays within the time period we reviewed.
- *Economic*: Includes changes that are driven by the economy (e.g., inflation, interest rates, real GDP, market prices, and the unemployment rate).
- *Technical*: Includes changes related to legislation that was passed *prior* to the formulation of original budget estimates, revisions to estimation models, some factors related to the performance of the economy (e.g., capital gains realizations), and any other changes that were not clearly driven by subsequent legislation or changes in the economic forecast.

Source: GAO analysis.

Figure 7. Factors Affecting Budget Estimates

Table 1 summarizes the factors—legislative, economic, and technical—that most significantly resulted in differences between estimated and actual outlays by fiscal year and account. The factors that were major drivers for differences between estimated and actual outlays are denoted with "√." Other factors that affected the difference are denoted with "x." In one case, it was unclear which factors most significantly caused the difference between estimated and actual outlays. In that case, both relevant factors are marked with an "x." Detailed explanations supporting this summary are presented in appendix I.

Table 1. Reasons for Differences between Estimated and Actual Outlays

Account	Reason for differences			
	Fiscal year	**Legislative**	**Reason for differences Economic**	**Technical**
Commodity Credit Corporation—Corn	2000	√	x	
	2001	√	x	x
	2002		√	
	2003	√	x	
	2004		√	x
Commodity Credit Corporation—Crop Disaster Assistance	2000	√		
	2001	√		
	2002	√		
	2003	√		
	2004	√		
Federal Direct Student Loan Program Account	2000			√
	2001		√	x
	2002		√	x
	2003		√	x
	2004			√
Grants to States for Medicaid	2000			√
	2001			√
	2002			√
	2003	√		x
	2004	√		x
Medicare Part A—Federal Hospital Insurance Trust Fund	2000			√
	2001			√
	2002			√
	2003		x	x
	2004	√		x

Table 1. (Continued)

Account	Reason for differences			
	Fiscal year	**Legislative**	**Reason for differences Economic**	**Technical**
Medicare Part B—Federal Supplementary Medical Insurance Trust Fund	2000			√
	2001			√
	2002			√
	2003	√	x	x
	2004	√		x
Rail Industry Pension Fund	2000			√
	2001			√
	2002	√		x
	2003	√		x
	2004	√		x
Unemployment Trust Fund	2000		√	
	2001		√	
	2002	√	x	
	2003	√	x	
	2004	√	x	
Total major drivers of differences		**19**	**7**	**13**

Source: GAO analysis of agencies' explanations of differences between estimated and actual outlays.

Note: Factors that were major drivers for the difference between estimated and actual outlays are denoted with "√" Other factors that affected the difference are denoted with "x." In one case, it was unclear which factors most significantly affected the difference. In that case, both relevant factors are marked with an "x."

Legislation Enacted After Original Estimates Explained Many Differences between Estimated and Actual Outlays

As seen above in table 1, most of the accounts we reviewed were directly affected by legislation that was enacted after original estimates were developed and significantly contributed to differences between expected and actual outlays in 19 out of 40 instances.[32] For example, the Temporary Extended Unemployment Compensation Act (TEUC) of 2002 led to the disbursement of greater-than-expected unemployment benefits. Supplemental appropriations for crop disaster assistance and Agricultural Market Transition Act payments largely contributed to additional outlays that were not assumed in original CCC budget projections. Similarly, the MMA and the Railroad Retirement and Survivors' Improvement Act of 2001, respectively, increased Medicare outlays and Rail Industry Pension outlays.

TEUC was enacted to provide up to 13 weeks of federally funded unemployment insurance benefits to workers in all states who had exhausted their entitlement to regular state unemployment benefits. Furthermore, the Act provided up to 13 additional weeks of federally funded benefits to workers in states with especially high unemployment rates. Congress renewed this extension in April 2003, which allowed qualified individuals to file for federal extensions through December 2003 and collect on those extensions through December 2004. As a result, program outlays exceeded estimates by $7.9 billion in 2002, $11 billion in 2003, and $4.3 billion in 2004.

Outlays in both CCC programs that we reviewed also were directly affected by subsequent legislative action that occurred after original budget estimates were formulated. For example, Crop Disaster Assistance programs are funded through supplemental appropriations every year throughout the 5-year period that we reviewed, which led to an additional total of $6 billion in program outlays. According to OMB officials, the Administration prefers not to include estimates in the budget for relatively unpredictable disaster-related programs such as crop disaster assistance. Instead, such funding is typically initiated by Congress through supplemental appropriations.[33] Accordingly, for all 5 years we examined, no estimates were provided and all of the outlays were as a result of supplemental appropriations.

Legislative action that increased market loss assistance payments to corn producers largely contributed to the greatest underestimates of outlays for that particular commodity—nearly $9 billion in 2000 and 2001 together. These payments were authorized on an ad hoc basis and, in fiscal year 2000, were paid out for both 1999 and 2000.

The Consolidated Appropriations Resolution of 2003 provided substantially higher Medicare[34] payments to physicians than estimated in original budget projections and contributed to the largest discrepancy—over $13 billion—between estimated and actual SMI outlays throughout the 5 years that we reviewed. Furthermore, both the HI and SMI trust funds incurred unanticipated additional outlays as a result of MMA. Several of the provisions under MMA were implemented in 2004 and directly affected that year's outlays; however, officials from the Centers for Medicare & Medicaid Services (CMS) said that the largest factors that led to additional HI outlays of approximately $4.4 billion and additional SMI outlays of nearly $12.3 billion were the substantially increased payments to private health plans and rural health providers, as well as the increased physician payment update—all of which were provided for under MMA.

Finally, the Railroad Retirement and Survivors' Improvement Act of 2001 changed a number of benefit and eligibility criteria, which led to a sharp rise in retirements. For example, the enactment of this law (1) eliminated benefit reductions to early retirees, (2) eliminated the maximum threshold on the amount of combined monthly employee and spouse benefit payments, (3) lowered the minimum eligibility requirement for railroad retirement annuities, and (4) increased benefit payments for widow(er)s. Under this legislation, funds in excess of those needed for current benefit payments and administrative expenses were transferred to the National Railroad Retirement Investment Trust. As a result, rail industry retirements increased, and pension fund outlays increased by almost $20 billion in 2002 and 2003 collectively.

Economic Factors Were Especially Important in Some Programs' Differences

Case study agencies cited economic factors as primary reasons for differences between estimated and actual outlays for 7 out of 40 differences. This was especially true for agricultural commodities, student loans, and unemployment insurance. For example, market prices for commodities affected federal subsidy payments to farmers, changes in interest rates affected revenues received from student loan borrowers, and unemployment affected outlays of federal unemployment insurance. Economic factors also affected the hospital market basket, which contributed to greater-than-expected Medicare outlays.

For CCC's corn program,[35] market prices were both underestimated and overestimated over the 5-year period. According to a Department of Agriculture (USDA) official, corn prices are extremely volatile and highly dependent on weather conditions and global food production. In addition, the countercyclical design of federal commodity subsidies results in outlays that are highly sensitive to changes in price. This official explained that a 1 cent change in estimated corn prices results in about an $85 million change in federal outlays.

The historically low interest rates that prevailed in recent years were below levels previously forecasted, which affected estimated student loan subsidy costs. Subsidy cost estimates for FDLP are highly sensitive to changes between projected and actual interest rates because borrower interest rates are variable. The decline in interest rates resulted in lower-than-expected interest payments to the government from FDLP borrowers, thus increasing reestimated subsidy costs for these loans.[36] Concurrently, the volume of student consolidation loans, which allow borrowers to lock in fixed interest rates, increased as interest rates declined. In consolidating their loans, borrowers effectively paid off their underlying loans, thereby lowering anticipated interest payments to the government on the loans and, in turn, increasing the estimated subsidy costs of the underlying loans.

Discrepancies between estimated and actual unemployment insurance outlays are partially attributed to economic factors such as unanticipated changes in both the unemployment rate and benefit recipiency rates. For example, Department of Labor officials said that most of the outlay overestimate in 2000 resulted from a lower-than-expected unemployment rate—the ratio of the total number of unemployed individuals to the total workforce—which translated into lower-than-expected outlays. In subsequent years, the unemployment rate was underestimated and thus contributed to greater-than-expected outlays. Inaccurate assumptions about the benefit recipiency rates, that is, the ratio of the total number of unemployed individuals filing for or receiving benefits to the total number of unemployed, further contributed to the agency's errors in accurately estimating program outlays. According to agency officials, these economic factors tend to be key drivers affecting budget estimates, albeit to a somewhat lesser degree during the timeframe we reviewed given the significance of the temporary extended unemployment compensation legislation that substantially increased outlays in 2002 through 2004.

To a lesser extent, economic factors affected Medicare outlays. In 2003, a higher-than-expected market basket,[37] which is basically a price index representing the cost of providing health care services to patients, was part of the explanation behind higher-than-originally-estimated Medicare outlays, according to CMS officials. This increase in the market basket led to greater-than-expected inpatient and outpatient hospital expenditures in the HI and SMI funds respectively.

Technical Factors Explained a Broad Spectrum of Differences

Technical factors, which encompass a somewhat wide-ranging residual category, significantly explained outlay differences in 13 out of 40 instances. Generally, technical factors account for differences between budget estimates and actual outlays that cannot be attributed to legislative or economic factors. For example, delayed implementation and difficulty in predicting the behavior of providers under new payment systems, an increased case mix, and the deferral of adjusting payments for skilled nursing facilities utilization led to differences between estimated and actual Medicare outlays. Increases in administrative costs and revised assumptions of the amount of loan defaults and collections caused some of the direct student loan outlays to differ from original estimates. Similar to the diversity of the programs we reviewed, there was great variability among the technical factors that affected account outlays.

Actual outlays for both Medicare Parts A and B differed from estimates primarily due to a number of technical factors, which accounted for both some of the largest and some of the smallest discrepancies. For example, the largest discrepancy in the HI fund (Medicare Part A) occurred in fiscal year 2000 for which outlays were lower-than-originally estimated by nearly $16 billion. According to CMS, the majority of this inaccuracy is attributed to lower-than-expected benefit payments as a result of the agency's difficulty in predicting the behavior of providers under newly implemented payment systems for skilled nursing facility (SNF) services and home health services. CMS officials said that these payment systems were very new at the time fiscal year 2000 budget estimates were done and the effect of these new systems was unknown. Similarly, SMI outlays were $4.6 billion less-than-originally estimated due largely to the delayed implementation of and unfamiliarity with a new outpatient hospital prospective payment system. Other technical factors CMS cited to explain the differences between estimated and actual Medicare outlays included case mixes that were more complex than expected and deferred payment refinements for SNF utilization. Case mix refers to the average complexity of inpatient admissions for Medicare beneficiaries. A change in the mix of cases causes the amount of benefit payments to change. The deferral of payment adjustments for SNF utilization contributed to greater-than-expected outlays in both fiscal years 2003 and 2004. These adjustments would have reduced payment rates that had previously been increased on a temporary basis under the Medicare, Medicaid, and SCHIP Balanced Budget Refinement Act of 1999 (BBRA).[38] CMS included the budgetary effects of these adjustments in their HI estimates for 2003 and 2004, but later decided not to implement them citing the need for additional time to review and analyze the implications of implementing hospital case mix refinements.

Differences between estimated and actual outlays for federal direct student loans were most frequently explained by technical factors, including revised assumptions in the Department of Education's loan subsidy model, increased administrative costs, and Congress's decision not to adopt a budget proposal to shift administrative expenses to a discretionary account. Moreover, because of the way federal credit programs are budgeted, original estimates include a loan subsidy amount for one fiscal year but actual outlays include a loan subsidy reestimate for all prior fiscal years—in the case of FDLP, up to 8 years for fiscal year 2004.

CONCLUSIONS

Given that unsustainable federal deficits and debt threaten our future economy and national security as well as the standard of living for the American people, renewed emphasis on increasing fiscal discipline is crucial. Mandatory spending represents an increasing percentage of the federal budget (e.g., about 54 percent in 2004, up from about 42 percent in 1984). Unexpected growth in individual programs—especially certain very large programs—can significantly change the nation's fiscal position. By identifying significant increases in mandatory spending relatively early and acting to constrain it, Congress may avert even larger fiscal challenges in the future.

The notion of establishing budget triggers to constrain growth is not new and has been used in the past with varying degrees of success. Given that spending for mandatory programs is driven by underlying benefit and eligibility formulas, serious efforts to constrain spending would require substantive changes to current law. Such changes should consider program goals and objectives and be enacted as programs are created, reexamined, or reauthorized. While budget triggers certainly are neither a panacea nor a substitute for deliberate consideration by stakeholders and decision makers, they can help to prompt action and enhance fiscal responsibility.

Ignoring significant growth in mandatory accounts is inconsistent with evaluation of programs and their costs. While we appreciate the concerns raised by budget experts, in our opinion, establishing budget triggers warrants serious consideration in order to constrain growth in mandatory spending programs. However, it is clear that how the triggers are designed must be carefully

5considered. For example, once widespread agreement on underlying public policy goals has been achieved, it needs to be decided whether a soft or hard response to a trigger—or a combination thereof—would be most appropriate. Also, it is important to consider the data upon which the trigger will hinge—future projections of historical data, growth as a percent of GDP, total growth, or another measure altogether. Moreover, this trigger concept might also be useful in examining tax expenditure growth. Calculating a normal range of uncertainty for a program could help avoid triggering an action prematurely or unnecessarily. In addition, it is important to strike an appropriate balance between responses that constrain spending or increase revenues. We recognize that automatic responses pose much more difficult trade-offs. Ensuring countercyclical effects are not undermined is of particular importance. In any case, recognizing the natural tension in balancing both long-term fiscal challenges and other public policy goals, each program needs to be considered individually to ensure that any responses triggered strike the appropriate balance between the long-term fiscal challenge and the program goals. Considering ways to increase transparency, oversight, and control of mandatory spending programs must be part of addressing the nation's long-term fiscal challenges.

MATTER FOR CONGRESSIONAL CONSIDERATION

To promote explicit scrutiny of significant growth in mandatory accounts, as mandatory spending programs are created, reexamined, or reauthorized, Congress should consider incorporating budget triggers that would signal the need for action. Further, it should determine whether in some cases it might be appropriate to consider automatically causing some action to be taken when the trigger is exceeded. Once a trigger is tripped, Congress could either accept or reject all or a portion of the response to the spending growth.

APPENDIX I: ILLUSTRATIVE EXAMPLES OF TRIGGERS AND RESPONSES FOR CASE STUDY ACCOUNTS

Addressing growth in mandatory spending is an important but complicated matter that requires looking below the aggregate and into specific programs. Mandatory spending is governed by eligibility rules and benefit formulas, which means that funds are spent as required to meet the needs of all those who are eligible and wish to participate. Accordingly, spending in mandatory programs cannot be constrained through the application of simple caps/limits. Rather, it requires changes in the underlying benefit structure and design of programs. As a result, constraints of individual programs that look at the specific economic and other factors that drive spending are likely to be most effective.

One idea to constrain growth in mandatory programs is to develop triggers that, when tripped, would cause some automatic cost-cutting or revenue-increasing response—such as changes in eligibility criteria, benefit formulas, or fees—automatically to go into effect unless Congress and the President act to make other changes. An alternative approach would replace such a "hard" response with a "soft" one such as requiring special consideration of a program or a proposal for action when the trigger's threshhold is breached. Examples of soft responses include raising a point of order, requiring the administering agency to prepare a special report explaining why the trigger was breached, or submitting a proposal for reform. Soft responses may be helpful in alerting decision makers of potential problems but do not ensure that such action is taken.

Especially in designing hard responses, careful consideration must be given to avoid counteracting the program's goals and objectives. For example, a rise in the unemployment rate would by design increase outlays in federal unemployment insurance not only to provide assistance to the unemployed but also to stabilize the economy. If a trigger were established that resulted in a contractionary response, it could undermine these important goals and exacerbate the effects of unemployment on the economy.

We selected seven mandatory budget accounts to examine in order to inform our thinking about budget trigger responses and the design issues that need to be considered. These seven accounts were selected because of their relatively large 5-year average differences between estimated and actual outlays. These accounts are the

(1) Commodity Credit Corporation[39]
  - Corn
  - Crop Disaster Assistance,

(2) Federal Direct Student Loan Program Account,
(3) Grants to States for Medicaid,
(4) Medicare Part A: Federal Hospital Insurance Trust Fund,
(5) Medicare Part B: Federal Supplementary Medical Insurance Trust Fund,
(6) Rail Industry Pension Fund, and
(7) Unemployment Trust Fund.

In this appendix, for each case study account we present contextual information such as the administering agency, program description, and source of funding. Also we provide the agency's explanation of key differences between estimated and actual outlays and, as appropriate, other relevant information. Finally, where appropriate we present illustrative examples of hard responses that could be established to constrain spending.[40] In some cases these illustrative examples involve revising currently existing triggers and their corresponding actions. In other cases new triggers and responses are presented. We do not specifically advocate any of these approaches as Congress would need to balance the program and national objectives sought with the long-term fiscal challenges facing our nation. The approaches we present are for illustrative purposes only to provide a sense of the types of trigger and resulting actions that could be established.

Account Name

Commodity Credit Corporation Fund—Corn

Administering Organization

Primarily the Farm Service Agency (FSA), U.S. Department of Agriculture

Program Description

The Commodity Credit Corporation (CCC) is a government-owned and government-operated entity that was created in 1933 to stabilize, support, and protect farm income and prices. CCC also helps maintain balanced and adequate supplies of agricultural commodities and aids in their orderly distribution.

For fiscal years 2000–2002 (under 1996 Farm Bill provisions), CCC provided corn-related subsidies primarily through two types of payments available to supplement farmers' incomes: (1) production flexibility payments to historical producers of corn and (2) nonrecourse loans, which allow farmers to store production and use loan proceeds to meet cash flow needs without selling the crop. Ad hoc legislation provided additional payments in the form of market loss assistance payments to compensate producers for low prices.

For fiscal years 2003–2004 (under 2002 Farm Bill provisions), CCC provided corn-related subsidies through three types of payments available to supplement farmers' incomes: (1) direct payments to historical producers of corn; (2) countercyclical payments, which provide a safety net in the event of low crop prices; and (3) nonrecourse loans.

Funding Source

CCC has an authorized capital stock of $100 million held by the United States and the authority to have outstanding borrowings of up to $30 billion at any one time. Funds are borrowed from the U.S. Treasury.

Differences between Estimated and Actual Outlays

Based on a 5-year average, estimated outlays for corn differed from actual outlays by about $1.9 billion per year, or 63.4 percent, in absolute value terms. However, the actual annual differences varied between an overestimate of $388 million and an underestimate of $7 billion. Table 2 presents the estimated and actual outlays associated with CCC's corn program, by fiscal year.

Table 2. Estimated and Actual Corn Outlays, by Fiscal Year

Nominal dollars in millions			
Fiscal year	**Original outlay estimate**	**Actual outlays**	**Difference**
2000	$3,087	$10,136	$-7,049
2001	4,444	6,297	-1,853
2002	3,013	2,959	54
2003	1,803	1,415	388
2004	2,695	2,504	191
5-year average dollar difference			$-1,654
5-year average difference as a percent of average estimated outlays			-55.5%
5-year average dollar difference (absolute value)			$1,907
5-year percentage difference (absolute value)			63.4%

Source: GAO analysis of FSA budget data.

Table 3. Explanation of Differences between Estimated and Actual Corn Outlays

Nominal dollars in billions			
Fiscal year and dollar difference[a]	**FSA's explanation of differences**		
	Legislative	**Economic**	**Technical**
2000 $-7.0	Additional $5.1 billion fixed payments for producers of grains and cotton were authorized in Oct. 1999 (Pub. L. 106-78 § 802).	Loan deficiency payments were underestimated by $1.6 billion due to a sharp drop in prices ($0.20 and $0.25 per bushel for 1999 and 2000 projections). Remaining differrence due to lower loan repayments since more loans were repaid at lower rates due to weak market conditions, representing marketing loan gains for producers.	
2001 $-1.9	$2.1 billion Market Loss Assistance payments were authorized in Aug. 2001 (Pub. L. 107-25 § 1).	Underpayment was moderated by a small reduction in loan deficiency payments resulting from a slight rise in the average market price and a change in the seasonal pattern from projections.	A small drop in net loan expenditures, as less corn was placed under loan than projected.
2002 $0.05		Three cent per bushel drop in the 2001 price of corn, which triggered higher loan deficiency payments (LDP). As more producers opted for LDPs, fewer placed corn under loan, thus reducing net outlays.	
2003 $0.39	Mandated policy change saved $1.9 billion by elimi-nating production flexibil-ity contract payments unle-ss requested by producers who are parties to the cont-ract (Pub. L. 107-171 § 1107). This was partially offset by $1.4 billion for the new direct payment program.	Increase in net loan outlays, reflecti-ng a change in the loan rates. The rate for 2002 and 2003 corn was assumed at $1.67 per bushel under previous legislation but increased to $1.98 under 2002 legislation. Thus, the face value of loans made went up.	
2004 $0.19		An increase in prices pushed corn above the countercyclical payment (CCP) trigger level, thus reducing CCPs by $397 million. The CCP decline outweighed increases of $100 million for LDPs, which refl-ect a decline in the 2004 crop price, raising the LDP rate and quantity.	The CCP decline out-weighed increases of $130 million for direct payments, which were due to higher base acr-es than were assumed before the actual signup.

Source: Farm Service Agency.

Notes: Primary drivers of outlay differences are marked in bold.

[a] A negative difference means that actual outlays were higher than originally estimated. A positive difference means that actual outlays were less than originally estimated.

Explanation of Key Differences

According to the Farm Service Agency, legislative action and economic changes were the primary reasons behind differences between estimated and actual outlays for CCC's corn program during fiscal years 2000 through 2004. In general, weather and natural disasters are the key drivers of differences between estimated and actual outlays, which are highly sensitive to changes in the price of corn. Outlays increase when the corn price decreases. A 1 cent drop in the price of a bushel of corn can lead to about $85 million increase in countercyclical payments. Participation also affects costs. Farm program costs depend on market prices and farm production, which in turn are influenced by world weather, the condition of the general economy, the foreign and trade policies of the United States and other food-exporting nations, the rate of inflation, and the value of the dollar, among other variables. Detailed explanations are shown in table 3.

Illustrative Triggers and Response

The 2002 Farm Bill[41] guaranteed historical producers of corn and other commodities a minimum price per bushel, known as a target price, which they can expect to earn. To constrain spending, one possible trigger could be when the target price exceeds the market price by some historically average percentage, the legislated target price could be reduced. However, to avoid price shocks to the industry and possible procyclical effects, the price reduction could be deferred to the following year.

The Farm Bill also established a formula for fixed, direct payments to historical producers of corn and other commodities. To limit spending on this income-support program, one idea for a trigger could be to link direct payments to farm sector production prices. For example, if production prices drop by more than 3 percent,[42] Congress could redefine the formula to be less generous.

Alternatively, Congress could limit the guarantee of direct payments to current producers of corn rather than historical producers.

Account Name

Commodity Credit Corporation Fund—Crop Disaster Assistance

Administering Organization

Primarily the Farm Service Agency (FSA), U.S. Department of Agriculture

Program Description

CCC is a government-owned and government-operated entity that was created in 1933 to stabilize, support, and protect farm income and prices. CCC also helps maintain balanced and adequate supplies of agricultural commodities and aids in their orderly distribution.

Crop Disaster Assistance programs reimburse producers for qualifying losses to agricultural commodities (other than sugar cane or cotton seed) due to damaging weather or related conditions. The damages must be in excess of 35 percent of the established price of crops for lost production or 20 percent for lost quality. Crop disaster programs cover insured, uninsured, and noninsurable crops. The program has no set funding limitation, however, payments are limited to $80,000 per person, and producers with incomes greater than $2.5 million are ineligible. This crop disaster assistance program is not permanently authorized.

Funding Source

CCC has an authorized capital stock of $100 million held by the United States and the authority to have outstanding borrowings of up to $30 billion at any one time. Funds are borrowed from the U.S. Treasury. Although Crop Disaster Assistance programs are provided through appropriations acts,[43] the Department of Agriculture considers and applies funding for the programs in a manner similar to mandatory programs. According to an FSA official, funding is provided to all eligible applications for assistance by prorating available funding if necessary. The Office of Management and Budget (OMB) also considers crop disaster assistance programs to be mandatory in that all eligible applicants may receive benefits.

Table 4. Estimated and Actual Crop Disaster Assistance Outlays, by Fiscal Year

Nominal dollars in millions			
Fiscal year	**Original outlay estimate**	**Actual outlays**	**Difference**
2000	$0	$1,251	$-1,251
2001	0	1,848	-1,848
2002	0	230	-230
2003	0	1,867	-1,867
2004	0	804	-804
5-year average dollar difference			$-1,200
5-year average difference as a percent of average estimated outlays			N/A
5-year average dollar difference (absolute value)			$1,200
5-year percentage difference (absolute value)			N/A

Source: GAO analysis of FSA budget data.

Differences between Estimated and Actual Outlays

Based on a 5-year average, estimated outlays for crop disaster assistance differed from actual outlays by about $1.2 billion per year in absolute value terms. However, the actual annual differences varied between $230 million and $1.9 billion. Table 4 presents the estimated and actual outlays associated with CCC's crop disaster assistance programs, by fiscal year.

Explanation of Key Differences

According to OMB staff, it is not OMB's policy to include an estimate for disaster assistance in the President's budget. Instead, these programs are typically funded through subsequent legislation.

Ideas for Improving the Accuracy of Estimates

Although OMB typically does not include an estimate for crop disaster assistance in the President's budget, we have reported in the past that shifting the budget timing to an up-front recognition of emergency costs through reserves may promote a more comprehensive and transparent debate over federal budgetary priorities during the regular budget process.[44] For example, we suggested that federal governmentwide emergency reserves could set aside budget authority in advance for expected yet unpredictable events as part of the annual resource-allocation process. Another approach would be to establish agency-specific reserve funds for those agencies that regularly respond to federal emergencies. Funds would be appropriated to these agencies on a contingent basis, meaning that certain agency-specific criteria would have to be met before the funds could be used. While these approaches are not of the trigger/response variety that is the subject of this chapter, they would help accomplish a goal of constraining spending if the emergency budget authority provided in advance is assumed to be within a constrained total budget authority.

Account Name

Federal Direct Student Loan Program Account

Administering Organization

Office of Federal Student Aid, U.S. Department of Education

Program Description

The Department of Education (Education) provides financial aid in part to increase access to college. Education's first direct loans were made in the fourth quarter of fiscal year 1994.[45] Through its William D. Ford Federal Direct Loan Program (FDLP), students and/or their parents borrow money directly from the federal government through the vocational, undergraduate, or graduate schools the students attend. As is the case under the Federal Family Education Loan Program (FFELP), or "guaranteed" student loan program, there are four types of direct loans.[46]

Stafford Loans—variable rate loans available to students. The federal government pays the interest on behalf of borrowers while the student is in school, during a 6-month grace period when the student first leaves school, and during statutory deferment periods related to borrower unemployment and economic hardship.

Unsubsidized Stafford Loans—variable rate loans to students with the same terms as Stafford Loans except that the government does not pay interest costs during in-school, grace, and deferment periods.

PLUS Loans—variable rate loans made to parents. The borrower pays all interest costs.

Consolidation Loans—borrowers may combine multiple federal student loans into a single, fixed rate loan. The interest rate is based on the weighted average of the interest rates in effect on the loans being consolidated or a fixed percentage.

Funding Source

Education finances FDLP through a combination of appropriations and borrowing from Treasury. Education receives permanent, indefinite budget authority for estimated subsidy costs—the amount expected not to be repaid by borrowers—of its loans. These costs are generally updated, or reestimated, annually. The portion of direct loans that Education predicts will ultimately be repaid by borrowers is financed by borrowing from Treasury and is not considered a cost to the government because it is expected to be returned to the government in future years.

Differences between Estimated and Actual Outlays

Based on a 5-year average, estimated outlays for direct student loans differed from actual outlays by about $2.6 billion per year, or 702 percent, in absolute value terms. However, the actual annual differences varied between an overestimate of $2.8 billion and an underestimate of $5.3 billion. A large component of these differences reflects the fact that initial estimates do not include reestimates of prior year costs, which are reflected in actual outlays. In addition, initial estimates reflect proposed policies, many of which were not enacted and so were not reflected in subsequent actual outlays. Table 5 presents the estimated and actual outlays associated with the federal direct student loan program, by fiscal year.

Explanation of Key Differences

Because FDLP is a relatively new program, it has a short history of repayment activity and little historical data are available. Accordingly, Education initially relied heavily on data from the guaranteed student loan program to develop estimates for most key cash flow assumptions in its FDLP cash flow model, which is used to estimate the subsidy cost of the program. Over the past few years, Education has incorporated FDLP data into many cash flow assumptions; as more data become available, Education plans to completely phase out the use of guaranteed loan data for FDLP assumptions.[47]

Table 5. Estimated and Actual Direct Student Loan Outlays, by Fiscal Year

Nominal dollars in millions			
Fiscal year	**Original outlay estimate**	**Actual outlays**	**Difference**
2000	$-42	$-2,862	$2,820
2001	115	257	-142
2002	-635	97	-732
2003	-283	5,055	-5,338
2004	-786	3,246	-4,032
5-year average dollar difference			$-1,485
5-year average difference as a percent of average estimated outlays			455.2%
5-year average dollar difference (absolute value)			$2,613
5-year percentage difference (absolute value)			702%

Source: GAO analysis of President's budget data.

Note: A negative outlay amount indicates a positive collection of revenue. Also, for credit programs, the term actual is misleading because reestimates will continue until all the loans in that cohort have been repaid.

Drops in interest rates have been a key driver behind differences in estimated versus actual outlays. Not only are loans being paid off at lower rates than anticipated but the drop in rates has also led to a dramatic increase in consolidations (which are prepayments). Detailed explanations are shown in table 6.

Table 6. Explanation of Differences between Estimated and Actual Direct Student Loan Outlays

Nominal dollars in billions			
Fiscal year and dollar differences[a]	**Education's explanation of differences**		
	Legislative	**Economic**	**Technical**
2000 $2.8			Actual includes about $2.4 billion in prior year reestimates of loans made in fiscal years (FY) 1994 through 1999. Net downward reestimate of prior cohorts primarily due to revised assumptions about a drop in defaults and an increase in collections. FY 2000 cohort subsidy decreased $442 million. Administrative costs decreased $30 million.
2001 $-0.14		Changes in interest rates resulted in $481 million up-ward reestimate of prior year cohorts.	Actual includes about $481 million in prior year reestimates of loans made in FYs 1994 through 2000. FY 2001 cohort subsidy decreased $432 million. Admin-istrative costs increased $94 million
2002 $-0.73		Drop in interest rates caused FY 2002 cohort subsidy to increase $694 million due to lower projected borrower repayments.	Administrative costs increased $42 million.
2003 $-5.3		Revised assumptions on interest rates, prepayments through consolidations, and defaults resulted in upward reestimate of prior year cohorts of $4.6 billion. FY 2003 cohort subsidy incre-ased $250 million.	Actual includes about $4.6 billion for 2-years worth of prior-year reestimates of loans made in FYs 1994 through 2002. (No reestimate was executed in FY 2002.) $15 million policy proposal to shift administrative expenses to a discretionary account not enacted by Congress.
2004 $-4.0			$710 million policy proposal to shift administrative expenses to a discretionary account not enacted by Congress. About $2.6 billion in upward reestimates of prior year cohorts (loans made during FYs 1994 through 2003) reflects technical changes to model assumptions, including higher level of prepayments, which lower future interest income, and higher defaults for borrowers choosing income-contingent loan repayment.

Source: Department of Education.

Notes: Primary drivers of outlay differences are marked in bold.

[a] A negative difference means that actual outlays were higher than originally estimated. A positive difference means that actual outlays were less than originally estimated.

Illustrative Trigger and Response

Congress could decrease the subsidy cost to the government by, among other things, increasing the amount of fees borrowers must pay to obtain a loan or increasing borrowers' interest rate. For example, continued differences between estimated and actual outlays could be used as a trigger, resulting in higher origination fees or interest rates for new FDLP loans. In implementing such a trigger and response, Congress would need to consider whether FFELP borrowers should similarly be affected. Under current law, loans made to borrowers, unless otherwise specified, are to have the same terms, conditions, and benefits and be made available in the same amounts under both FDLP and FFELP.[48]

Account Name

Grants to States for Medicaid

Administering Organization

Centers for Medicare & Medicaid Services (CMS), U.S. Department of Health and Human Services

Program Description

Medicaid is a health-financing program for eligible low-income individuals and families. Federal statute defines over 50 population groups that are potentially eligible for states' programs. In general, eligibility is limited to low-income children, pregnant women, parents of dependent children, people with disabilities, and the elderly. Although Medicaid is one federal program, it consists of 56 distinct state-level programs—one for each state, territory, Puerto Rico, and the District of Columbia.[49] Each of the states has a designated Medicaid agency that administers the program. In accordance with the Medicaid statute and within broad federal guidelines, each state establishes its own eligibility standards; determines the type, amount, duration, and scope of covered services; sets payment rates; and develops its administrative structure.

Funding Source

The federal government matches state Medicaid spending for medical assistance according to a formula that compares each state's average per capita income—a proxy reflecting the health of the state's economy and its response to economic changes—to the national per capita income. Therefore, states with a high per capita income receive less federal funds than states with a low per capita income. As economic conditions improve or decline in a particular state, so does the amount of federal matching funds granted to that state. The federal share, known as the Federal Medical Assistance Percentage (FMAP), can range from 50 to 83 percent. States are required to describe the nature and scope of their programs in comprehensive written plans submitted to CMS—with federal funding for state Medicaid services contingent upon CMS approval of the plans. This approval hinges on whether CMS determines that state plans meet all applicable federal laws and regulations.

Although the source of Medicaid funding is through an annual appropriation act, Medicaid is not considered a discretionary spending program. Because Medicaid is an entitlement created by the operation of law, if Congress fails to appropriate money necessary to fund payments and benefits, eligible recipients may seek legal recourse. In such case, necessary payments may be made through the indefinite judgment fund pursuant to 31 U.S.C. § 1304.

Differences between Estimated and Actual Outlays

Based on a 5-year average, estimated Medicaid outlays differed from actual outlays by about $4.2 billion per year, or 2.9 percent, in absolute value terms. Actual annual differences ranged from an underestimate of $5.1 billion to an overestimate of $6.3 billion. Table 7 presents the estimated and actual Medicaid outlays for fiscal years 2000 through 2004.

Explanation of Key Differences

Both legislative and technical factors led to differences in estimated and actual Medicaid outlays. For example, the Jobs and Growth Tax Relief Reconciliation Act of 2003,[50] which temporarily changed federal matching rates for benefits and provided fiscal relief to states, affected estimated Medicaid outlays in both fiscal years 2003 and 2004. Technical factors included misestimates of medical assistance payments, administrative costs, vaccines for children, and collections. Also, there were a number of legislative proposals that were not adopted. It is not clear if economic factors also contributed to the differences, although it is likely so given the economic downturn that occurred during this time period. Changing economic conditions could have led to differences in the number of individuals eligible for and receiving benefits, and therefore total program outlays.

According to CMS officials, Medicaid estimates are based primarily on state estimates and may be adjusted by CMS' Office of the Actuary to reflect recent trends in how state estimates have changed over time or how they have compared with actual expenditures in recent years. Agency officials were unable to accurately identify and quantify the effects of any of these factors and explained that the difficulty lies with the variability of program structure across states. Each state is allowed the discretion to structure and modify its program, including the establishment of eligibility criteria and payment rates. Similarly, state legislative actions and economic conditions vary across the country and could have varying effects on program outlays. Consequently, aggregating state data into a single Medicaid figure would mask estimating inaccuracies and challenges since the negative effect in one might be offset by positive effect in another. In the event that the difference between estimated and actual spending is very large, CMS said it would then investigate and seek explanations from the states. Although CMS did not consider the differences evident throughout the 5-year period we reviewed to be large enough to prompt such an evaluation, they did provide some explanation behind misestimates as shown in table 8 below.

Table 7. Estimated and Actual Medicaid Outlays, by Fiscal Year

Nominal dollars in millions			
Fiscal year	**Original outlay estimate**	**Actual outlays**	**Difference**
2000	$114,660	$117,921	$-3,261
2001	124,838	129,374	-4,536
2002	142,423	147,512	-5,089
2003	158,790	160,693	-1,903
2004	182,543	176,231	6,312
5-year average dollar difference			$-1,695
5-year average difference as a percent of average estimated outlays			-1.2%
5-year average dollar difference (absolute value)			$4,220
5-year percentage difference (absolute value)			2.9%

Source: GAO analysis of President's budget data.

Table 8. Explanation of Differences between Estimated and Actual Medicaid Outlays

Nominal dollars in billions			
Fiscal year and dollar difference[a]	**CMS' explanation of differences**		
	Legislative	**Economic**	**Technical**
2000 -$3.3			Underestimated medical assistance payments by over $3 billion, administrative costs by $71 million, and vaccines for children by $2 million. The resulting outlay underestimate was further increased by a legislative proposal expected to save $161 million that had been included in the original estimate but was not accepted.
2001 -$4.6			Underestimated medical assistance payments by $7.1 billion and vaccines for children by $357 million. These underestimates were partially offset by a $977 million overestimate of administrative costs, an underestimate of almost $1.3 billion in collections, and a legislative proposal expected to cost $663 million that had been included in the original estimate but was not accepted.
2002 -$5.1			Underestimated medical assistance payments by $5.3 billion. This underestimate was partia-lly offset by a $138 million underestimate of collections and overestimates of administerative costs and vaccines for children by $722 million and $4 million respectively. The resulting outlay underestimate was further increased by a legislative proposal expected to save $606 million that had been included in the original estimate but was not accepted.
2003 -$1.9	The Jobs and Growth Tax Relief Reconciliation Act of 2003 was enacted in late May 2003, after original FY 2003 estimates were made. CMS said this legis-lation accounted for app-oimately $4 billion in unanticipated outlays.		Underestimated medical assistance payments by nearly $3 billion and vaccines for children by $241 million. These underestimates were partially offset by a $1.1 billion overestimate of administrative costs, a $112 million underestimate of collections, and a legislative proposal expected to cost $98 million that had been included in the original estimate but was not accepted.
2004 $6.3	The Jobs and Growth Tax Relief Reconciliation Act of 2003 was enacted in late May 2003, after original FY 2004 estimates were made. CMS said		Outlays were overestimated as a result of a legislative proposal expected to cost $5.8 billion, which had been included in the original estimate but was not adopted, a $1 billion overestimate of administrative costs, and a $168 million

	this legisl-ation accounted for appro-ximately $6 billion in unanticipated outlays.		underes-timate of collections. The resulting outlay overest-imate was partially offset by underestimates of medical assistance payments and vaccines for children by $520 million and $133 million respectively.

Source: Centers for Medicare & Medicaid Services.

Notes: Primary drivers of outlay differences are marked in bold.

[a] A negative difference means that actual outlays were higher than originally estimated. A positive difference means that actual outlays were less than originally estimated.

Account Name

Federal Hospital Insurance (HI) Trust Fund (Medicare Part A)

Administering Organization

Centers for Medicare & Medicaid Services, U.S. Department of Health and Human Services

Program Description

The account funds the Medicare Part A program which partially covers the costs of, among other things, home health care, inpatient care in hospitals and skilled nursing facilities, and hospice care. Based on their work history, most U.S. citizens and permanent residents and their spouses are eligible for Medicare Part A if they are 65 years of age or older. Also, certain persons under 65 years old who are disabled or have end-stage renal disease are eligible for coverage. Enrollees or their spouses who have contributed to Medicare through payroll taxes for at least 10 years of employment are automatically enrolled at age 65 and need not pay premiums to receive coverage. Individuals who have not met this eligibility requirement may pay a monthly premium to purchase Part A coverage.[51]

Table 9. Estimated and Actual HI Outlays, by Fiscal Year

Nominal dollars in millions			
Fiscal year	**Original outlay estimate**	**Actual outlays**	**Difference**
2000	$143,898	$127,973	$15,925
2001	143,427	140,573	2,854
2002	144,674	145,606	-932
2003	147,295	151,308	-4,013
2004	159,750	164,136	-4,386
5-year average dollar difference			$1,890
5-year average difference as a percent of average estimated outlays			1.3%
5-year average dollar difference (absolute value)			$5,622
5-year percentage difference (absolute value)			3.8%

Source: GAO analysis of President's budget data.

Funding Source

The primary funding source for Medicare Part A comes from payroll taxes. Other relevant revenue sources include interest on investments in government securities held by the fund,[52] income from taxation of Old Age, Survivors, and Disability Insurance (Social Security) benefits, and premiums collected from voluntary participants.

Differences between Estimated and Actual Outlays

Based on a 5-year average, estimated Medicare Part A outlays differed from actual outlays by about $5.6 billion per year, or 3.8 percent, in absolute value terms. Actual annual differences ranged from an underestimate of $4.3 billion to an overestimate of $15.9 billion. Table 9 presents the estimated and actual HI outlays for fiscal years 2000 through 2004.

Explanation of Key Differences

Both legislative and technical factors led to differences between estimated and actual HI outlays. For example, the Medicare Prescription Drug, Improvement, and Modernization Act of 2003 (MMA)[53] led to greater-than-expected outlays in fiscal year 2004. Technical factors included difficulty in predicting the behavior of providers under new payment systems, misestimates of home health transfers to and from the Supplementary Medical Insurance (SMI) Trust Fund, and misestimates of service usage. Economic factors, specifically the hospital market basket, also contributed to differences. The hospital market basket is an input price index that represents the cost of the mix of goods and services that comprise routine, ancillary, and special-care unit inpatient hospital services. Detailed explanations of the differences are shown in table 10.

Currently Existing Program Trigger and Response

MMA established a trigger with a soft response to constrain growth in Medicare; it requires the President to submit a proposal to Congress for action if the Medicare Trustees determine in 2 consecutive years that the general revenue share[54] of Medicare is projected to exceed 45 percent during a 7-year projection period. To date, this threshold has not been breached and thus no response has been triggered. According to the 2005 Medicare Trustees' report, the trigger is expected to be breached in 2012, which falls within the 7-year projection period that will be covered in the 2006 Medicare Trustees' report. If the 45 percent threshold is projected to be breached again in the next consecutive 7-year projection period, the President will be required to propose legislation, within 15 days of submitting the fiscal year 2009 budget, to respond to the funding warning.

Illustrative Trigger and Response

Using the trigger of general revenue exceeding 45 percent in 2 consecutive years during a 7-year period, hard responses could also be developed. Possible responses are to adjust taxes, benefit formulas, or eligibility criteria. For example, Medicare payroll taxes could automatically be increased unless Congress took action to prevent the increase. Alternatively, reaching the trigger could cause automatic changes to benefit formulas or eligibility criteria, or a combination of benefit changes and tax increases. Of course congressional action could change the automatic response if it was deemed inappropriate at that time.

Table 10. Explanation of Differences between Estimated and Actual HI Outlays

Nominal dollars in billions			
Fiscal year and dollar Difference[a]	CMS' explanation of differences		
	Legislative	Economic	Technical
2000 $15.9			Overestimated benefit payments by $10.1 billion, which CMS attributed to its difficulty in predicting the behavior of providers under new payment systems for skilled nur-sing facility (SNF) services and home health services. Also, a $6.6 billion overestimate of home health transfers to the SMI fund[b] further widened the gap between estimated and actual outlays. CMS attributed this to discrepancies in implementing the payment system, particularly by home health agencies. Specifically, the cap on average per-bene-ficiary home health expenditures was treated as an absol-ute cap, thereby cutting services to patients requiring num-erous visits per episode of care. This resulted in unexpec-ted additional savings. The resulting outlay overestimate was partially offset by a legislative proposal expected to save $808 million that had been included in the original estimate but was not accepted.
2001 $2.9			Overestimated benefit payments by almost $3.9 billion, which CMS attributed to the discrepancy between what they assumed service usage to be and actual usage. Overe-stimates of $242 million in home health transfers to the SMI fund and $84 million in quality improvement organ-izations (QIO)[c] further added to the difference. The resul-ting outlay overestimate was partially offset by a $1.2 bil-lion quinquennial adjustment as required by law[d] and a legislative proposal expected to save $185 million that had been included in the original estimate but was not adopted.

Table 10. (Continued)

Nominal dollars in billions			
Fiscal year and dollar Difference[a]	**CMS' explanation of differences**		
	Legislative	**Legislative**	**Legislative**
2002 -$0.9			Underestimated benefit payments by $2.3 billion, which CMS attributed to the discrepancy between what they ass-umed service usage to be and actual usage. The resulting outlay underestimate was partially offset by overestimates of $1.3 billion and $77 million in home health transfers to the SMI fund and QIOs respectively.
2003 -$4.0		Inpatient hospital expenditures were higher than expected due to a higher-than-expected "market basket" payment update. Market basket refers to the input price index based on the cost of a particular type of health provider (e.g., hospital, skilled nursing facility, home health agency) to provide services to patients. By law these indexes are used to update Medicare payments.	Inpatient hospital expenditures were higher than expected also because of a hospital case mix increase. Case mix refers to the average complexity of inpatient admissions for Medicare ben-eficiaries. Payments are based on the type of case, so if the mix of cases changes, payments also change. Expenditures were also higher because expected SNF resource utilization group (RUG) refinements were not made, which would have reduced payments. SNFs received higher payments due to the introduction of a new administrative policy to adjust payment updates for past differences between actual and estimated market basket increases. The $7.3 billion underestimate in benefit payments was further increased by an $18 million underestimate of administrative costs, but was partially offset by overestimates of $2.8 billion in home health transfers to the SMI fund, $43 million in QIOs, and a legislative proposal expected to cost $410 million that was included in the original estimate but was not adopted.

Table 10. (Continued)

Nominal dollars in billions			
Fiscal year and dollar Difference[a]	**CMS' explanation of differences**		
	Legislative	**Legislative**	**Legislative**
2004 -$4.4	Underestimated benefit payments by $4.3 billion. CMS attributed this to several MMA provisions that were enacted and implemented after origin-nal estimates were made, which led to higher actual expenditures. In particu-lar, payments to private health plans contracting with Medicare were increased substantially as were payments to rural health providers.		Once again, expected SNF RUG refinements were not made, resulting in higher-than- estimated expenditures. Hospice expenditures were also higher than estimated. The $4.3 billion underestimate in benefit payments was further increased by underestimates of $23 million in QIOs and $17 million in administrative costs.

Source: Centers for Medicare & Medicaid Services.

Notes: Primary drivers of outlay differences are marked in bold. In 2003 it was unclear which factor most significantly affected the difference. In that case, there is no primary driver marked in bold.

[a] A negative difference means that actual outlays were higher than originally estimated. A positive difference means that actual outlays were less than originally estimated.

[b] Home health agency transfers occur between the HI and SMI trust funds and total billions of dollars throughout the 5-year period. However, the positive variance in one fund is equally offset by the negative variance in the other. As a result, when the Medicare trust funds are taken together, this intertrust fund activity has no cumulative impact on the federal surplus/deficit.

[c] Quality improvement organizations are groups of practicing doctors and other health care experts paid by the federal government to check and improve the care given to Medicare patients.

[d] Section 217(g) of the Social Security Act provides for periodic transfers between the general fund of the Treasury and the HI trust fund, if needed to adjust prior payments for the costs arising from wage credits granted for military service before 1957.

Account Name

Federal Supplementary Medical Insurance (SMI) TrustFund (Medicare Part B)

Administering Organization

Centers for Medicare & Medicaid Services, U.S. Department of Health and Human Services

Program Description

This account, also known as Medicare Part B, partially covers the cost of doctors' services, clinical laboratory services, outpatient hospital services, some physical and occupational therapy services, and some home health care. Eligibility requirements for Medicare Part B are similar to those for Part A. However, unlike for Medicare Part A, enrollment is voluntary. Enrollees must pay a monthly premium to receive Part B coverage. In 2005, premiums were $78.20 per month and the deductible was $110. Premium and deductible rates may change every year.

Most Part B services are paid based on a fee schedule. Physicians, the largest Part B service type, are paid under the sustainable growth rate (SGR) system,[55] which determines the increase in payments per service for the physician fee schedule for each year based on a statutory formula. Under the SGR system, actual physician-related spending is compared with target physician-related spending levels. If actual spending exceeds target spending, then future physician fee schedule updates are reduced.

Funding Source

SMI is financed from general revenues (approximately 75 percent) and beneficiary premiums (approximately 25 percent).

Differences between Estimated and Actual Outlays

Based on a 5-year average, estimated Medicare Part B outlays differed from actual outlays by about $6.4 billion per year, or 6.1 percent, in absolute value terms. Actual annual differences ranged from an underestimate of $13.4 billion to an overestimate of $4.6 billion. Table 11 presents the estimated and actual SMI outlays by fiscal year.

Table 11. Estimated and Actual SMI Outlays, by Fiscal Year

Nominal dollars in billions			
Fiscal year	**Original outlay estimate**	**Actual outlays**	**Difference**
2000	$91,795	$87,216	$4,579
2001	96,372	97,531	-1,159
2002	107,830	107,113	717
2003	108,416	121,816	-13,400
2004	119,353	131,632	-12,279
5-year average dollar difference			$-4,308
5-year average difference as a percent of average estimated outlays			-4.1%
5-year average dollar difference (absolute value)			$6,427
5-year percentage difference (absolute value)			6.1%

Source: GAO analysis of President's budget data.

Currently Existing Program Triggers and Responses

Congress has established two triggers with soft and hard responses to constrain growth in SMI. First, under the SGR system, if actual physician-related spending exceeds target physician-related spending then future physician fee schedule updates are reduced. Because the actual versus target spending comparison is cumulative, future fee updates are reduced to lower future actual spending below future target spending until total cumulative actual spending is the same as total cumulative target spending. Although the SGR system was designed to encourage fiscal discipline, Congress has chosen to modify or override this constraint a number of times. We have previously reported on concerns about the SGR system and considerations for reform.[56] Second, MMA established a trigger with a soft response; it requires the President to submit a proposal to Congress for action if the Medicare Trustees determine in 2 consecutive years that the general revenue share of Medicare is projected to exceed 45 percent during a 7-year projection period. To date, this threshold has not been breached and thus no response has been triggered. As mentioned in the Medicare Part A section of this appendix, the trigger is expected to be breached in 2012, which falls within the specified 7-year projection period that will be covered in the 2006 Medicare Trustees' report. If the 45 percent threshold is projected to be breached again in the next consecutive 7-year projection period, the President will be required to propose legislation, within 15 days of submitting the fiscal year 2009 budget, to respond to the funding warning.

Illustrative Trigger and Response

Using the trigger of general revenue exceeding 45 percent in 2 consecutive years during a 7-year period, hard responses could also be developed. Possible responses are to adjust premiums,[57] benefit formulas, or eligibility criteria. For example, Part B premiums could automatically be increased unless Congress took action to prevent the increase. Alternatively, reaching the trigger could cause automatic changes to benefit formulas or eligibility criteria, or a combination of benefit changes and premium increases. Of course congressional action could change the automatic response if it was deemed inappropriate at that time.

Account Name

Rail Industry Pension Fund

Administering Organization

Railroad Retirement Board (RRB)

Under the Railroad Retirement Act, retirement and disability annuities are paid to railroad workers with at least 10 years of service, or 5 years if performed after 1995. Annuities are also payable to spouses and divorced spouses of retired workers and to widow(er)s, surviving divorced spouses, remarried widow(er)s, children, and parents of deceased railroad workers. Qualified railroad retirement beneficiaries are covered by Medicare in the same way as Social Security beneficiaries.

Table 12. Explanation of Differences between Estimated and Actual SMI Outlays

Nominal dollars in billions			
Fiscal year and dollar difference[a]	CMS' explanation of differences		
	Legislative	Economic	Technical
2000 $4.6			Benefit payments were $11.6 billion lower than expected, which CMS attributed to the delayed implem-entation and difficulty in predicting the behavior of providers under a new outpatient hospital prospec-tive payment system. The system was being created from scratch and little research had been done on what type of system would work best. Original projections had an earlier start date, which caused higher expenditures to be estimated. This overestim-ate was further increased by overes-timates of $90 mill-ion and $17 million in transfers to Medicaid and QIOs respectively. The resulting overesti-mate was partially offset by a $6.6 billion over-estimate of home health transfers received from the HI fund and a legislative proposal expected to save $570 million that had been included in the original estimate but was not adopted.

Table 12. (Continued)

Nominal dollars in billions			
Fiscal year and dollar difference[a]	**CMS' explanation of differences**		
	Legislative	**Economic**	**Technical**
2001 -$1.2			Most of the difference is attributed to a legislative proposal expected to save $685 million that was not adopted. Benefit payments were $241 million greater than expected, which CMS attributed to the discrep-ancy between what they assumed service usage to be and actual usage. In addition, home health transfers received from the HI fund were $242 million less than expected.
2002 $0.7			Most of the difference resulted from a $2.1 billion overestimate of benefit payments, which CMS attributed to the discrepancy between what they assumed service usage to be and actual usage. This overestimate was partially offset by a $1.3 billion overestimate of home health transfers received from the HI fund and a $42 million underestimate of transfers to Medicaid.
2003 -$13.4	Consolidated Appropriations Resolution 2003 was passed after the original budget estimates, which caused a substantially higher physician fee update than estimated in the projections.	A higher hospital market basket (as mentioned in the Medicare Part A sect-ion) also caused higher-than-expected outpatient hospital expenditures.	The underestimate of benefit payments was further increased by a $112 million underestimate of transfers to Medicaid, but was partially offset by a legislative proposal expected to cost $70 million that was not adopted and a $16 million overestimate in QIOs.

Table 12. (Continued)

Nominal dollars in billions			
Fiscal year and dollar difference[a]	**CMS' explanation of differences**		
	Legislative	**Economic**	**Technical**
2004 -$12.3	As noted in the Medicare Part A section, MMA was passed in 2003 and some of its provisions were implemented in 2004, causing higher private plan and rural provider expenditures. Also, the physician fee update was much higher than had been originally estimated due to the MMA legislation that was enacted after the 2004 budget estimates were made. Consequently, benefit payments were $12.2 billion greater than expected.		The underestimate of benefit payments was further increased by a $168 million underestimate of transfers to Medicaid, but was partially offset by a legislative proposal expected to cost $55 million that was included in the original estimate but not adopted.

Source: Centers for Medicare & Medicaid Services.

Notes: Primary drivers of outlay differences are marked in bold.

[a] A negative difference means that actual outlays were higher than originally estimated. A positive difference means that actual outlays were less than originally estimated.

Railroad retirement benefits are calculated under a two-tier formula. Tier I is based on combined railroad retirement and Social Security credits, using Social Security benefit formulas. Tier II is based on railroad service only and is similar to the defined benefit pensions paid over-and-above Social Security benefits in other industries. In addition, some annuitants may also be qualified for supplemental benefits and vested dual benefits. Cost-of-living adjustments on the Tier I portion of annuities are paid similarly to those for Social Security. However, the adjustment for the Tier II portion is limited to 32.5 percent of the previous year's increase in the Consumer Price Index. Supplemental annuities and vested dual benefits are not subject to cost-of-living adjustments.

Funding Source

Payroll taxes paid by railroad employers and their employees are the primary source of funding for the railroad retirement benefit program. Corresponding to the two-tier benefit structure, railroad retirement taxes are levied on a two-tier basis. Railroad retirement Tier I payroll taxes are coordinated with Social Security taxes so that employees and employers pay Tier I taxes at the same rate as Social Security taxes. In addition, both employees and employers pay Tier II taxes, which are used to finance railroad retirement benefit payments over-and-above Social Security equivalent levels. These Tier II taxes are based on the ratio of certain asset balances to the sum of benefit payments and administrative expenses.

While the railroad retirement system has remained separate from the Social Security system, the two systems are closely coordinated with regard to earnings credits, benefit payments, and taxes. The financing of the two systems is linked through a financial interchange under which, in effect, the portion of railroad retirement annuities that is equivalent to Social Security benefits is coordinated with the Social Security system. The purpose of this financial coordination is to place the Social Security trust funds in the same position they would be in if railroad service were covered by the Social Security program instead of the railroad retirement program.

Starting in fiscal year 2002, revenues in excess of benefit payments are invested to provide additional trust fund income. The National Railroad Retirement Investment Trust (NRRIT), established by the Railroad Retirement and Survivors' Improvement Act of 2001, manages and invests railroad retirement assets. The trust is a tax-exempt entity independent from the federal government. Railroad retirement funds are invested in nongovernmental assets, as well as in governmental securities. Prior to the Act, investment of Railroad Retirement Account assets was limited to U.S. government securities.

Additional trust fund income is derived from revenues from federal income taxes on railroad retirement benefits, and appropriations from general Treasury revenues provided after 1974 as part of a phase-out of certain vested dual benefits.

Differences between Estimated and Actual Outlays

Based on a 5-year average, estimated outlays from the Rail Industry Pension Fund differed from actual outlays by about $4.1 billion per year, or 125.7 percent, in absolute value terms. The actual annual differences between estimated and actual outlays varied between an overestimate of $77 million and an underestimate of about $17.9 billion. The majority of the underestimate was a result of legislation that resulted in funds being transferred out of the account and into a nongovernmental investment trust fund. Table 13 presents the estimated and actual outlays associated with the Rail Industry Pension Fund, by fiscal year.

Table 13. Estimated and Actual Rail Industry Pension Fund Outlays, by Fiscal Year

Nominal dollars in millions			
Fiscal year	**Original outlay estimate**	**Actual outlays**	**Difference**
2000	$3,038	$2,961	$77
2001	3,044	2,967	77
2002	3,078	4,814	-1,736
2003	3,416	21,326	-17,910
2004	3,639	4,225	-586
5-year average dollar difference			$-4,016
5-year average difference as a percent of average estimated outlays			-123.8%
5-year average dollar difference (absolute value)			$4,077
5-year percentage difference (absolute value)			125.7%

Source: GAO analysis of President's budget data.

Explanation of Key Differences

The discrepancies between estimated and actual outlays in fiscal years 2002 through 2004 can be attributed to the enactment of the Railroad Retirement and Survivors' Improvement Act of 2001, which was signed into law on December

21, 2001. This legislation lowered eligibility requirements for annuitants and eliminated reductions that previously applied to annuities of 30-year employees retiring between ages 60 and 62. The law also lowered the minimum eligibility requirement to receive regular annuities from 10 to 5 years of service after 1995 and increased the Tier II amount paid to a widow(er) from 50 percent to 100 percent. Additionally, the maximum limit on monthly railroad retirement benefits was eliminated. The law reduced the Tier II tax rate on rail employers in 2002 and 2003, and in 2004 provided automatic Tier II tax rate adjustments for both employers and employees. Lastly, funds in excess of those needed for current payment of benefits and administrative expenses were transferred to the National Railroad Retirement Investment Trust.

Agency officials indicated that the level of employment in the rail industry is the most difficult factor to predict when estimating revenue because it directly affects payroll tax income. Employment only affects estimates in the long term, not short term. When reporting budget estimates to OMB, the agency uses middle-range estimates that assume employment will decrease gradually over time. Additionally, financial interchanges of the estimated allocation of benefits between the Railroad Retirement Account and Social Security Equivalent Benefit Account make it difficult to estimate exact outlays as they are continually changing. A detailed explanation of the differences is shown in table 14.

Table 14. Explanation of Differences between Estimated and Actual Rail Industry Pension Fund Outlays

Nominal dollars in billions			
Fiscal year and dollar difference[a]	RRB's explanation of differences		
	Legislative	Economic	Technical
2000 $0.08			Difference results from changes in the estimated allocation of benefits betw-een the Railroad Retirement Account and Social Security Equivalent Benefit Account. The actual allocation of bene-fits between these accounts for a given calendar year is not known until the financial interchange etermination is completed some 16 months after the end of a calendar year (which implies about 19 months after the end of the fiscal year ending in the given calendar year).

Table 14. (Continued)

Nominal dollars in billions			
Fiscal year and dollar difference[a]	**RRB's explanation of differences**		
	Legislative	**Economic**	**Technical**
2002 $-1.7	The number of retirements increased due to the enactment of the Railroad Retirement and Survivors' Improv-ement Act of 2001, which lowered eligibility requirements for annuitants and eliminated reductions that previously applied to annuities of 30-year employees retiring at age 60. The Act also lowered the minimum eligibility requirement to receive regular annuities from 10 to 5 years of service after 1995 and increased the Tier II amount paid to a wido-w(er) from 50 percent to 100 percent.		The original outlay estimates are for benefit payments only.
	Additionally, the maximum limit on monthly railroad retirement benefits was eliminated. The Act reduced the Tier II tax rate on rail employers in 2002 and 2003, and in 2004 prov-ided automatic Tier II tax rate adju-stments for both employers and employees. Funds in excess of those required for current payment of benefits and administrative expenses, $1.432 billion, were transferred to the NRRIT.		
2003 $-17.9	The number of retirements increased due to the enactment of the Railroad Retirement and Survivors' Impro-vement Act of 2001. Funds in excess of those required for current paym-ent of benefits and administrative expenses, $17.75 billion, were transf-erred to the NRRIT.		The original outlay estimates are for benefit payments only.
2004 $-0.59	Funds in excess of those required for current payment of benefits and administrative expenses, $586 million, were transferred to the NRRIT.		The original outlay estimates are for benefit payments only.

Source: Railroad Retirement Board.

Notes: Primary drivers of outlay differences are marked in bold.

[a] A negative difference means that actual outlays were higher than originally estimated. A positive difference means that actual outlays were less than originally estimated.

Illustrative Trigger and Response

If actual outlays exceeded estimates by more than the historical average, Congress could reduce retirement benefits across the board. For example, if estimated outlays historically differed from actual outlays by a specified percent, increases in outlays above that specified percent could automatically result in an across-the-board increase in retirement contributions or a cut in retirement benefits. To determine an appropriate threshold, rail officials would need to look at long-term historical differences to minimize the effects of events such as the legislative change in fiscal years 2002 and 2003.

Account Name

Unemployment Trust Fund

Administering Organization

Employment and Training Administration, U.S. Department of Labor
50 states, District of Columbia, Puerto Rico, and the Virgin Islands

Program Description

Unemployment insurance is designed to serve as a "counter-cyclical" remedy to the effects of recessions by putting more dollars in the pockets of the labor force, thereby increasing the demand for goods and services and stabilizing the U.S. economy.

The Unemployment Trust Fund (UTF) finances unemployment insurance—a joint federal-state program that provides temporary cash benefits to eligible workers who become unemployed through no fault of their own and helps to stabilize the economy in times of economic recession. Guided by federal law, unemployed workers must meet certain criteria set by their state in order to receive these benefits. Unemployment insurance is administered by state employees under state law.

Extended benefits are paid during periods of high state unemployment. Extended benefits are financed one-half by state payroll taxes and one-half by the federal unemployment payroll tax. The federal tax also pays for the cost of federal and state administration of unemployment insurance, labor-market information programs, veterans' employment services, and 97 percent of the costs of the employment service. States may receive repayable advances from the UTF when their balances in the fund are insufficient to pay benefits.

Federal unemployment payroll taxes accumulate in three accounts: (1) the Employment Security Administration Account (ESAA), which covers both federal and state administrative costs; (2) the Extended Unemployment Compensation Account (EUCA), which covers the federal share of extended unemployment benefits and has been used to fund temporary extended unemployment compensation benefits; and (3) the Federal Unemployment Account (FUA), which funds loans to insolvent state accounts. There is a statutory ceiling on the size of each of these accounts, the amounts of which are calculated each September. The ceiling for the ESAA account is 40 percent of the appropriated amounts during the fiscal year for which the ceiling is being calculated. For the EUCA and FUA accounts, this ceiling is 0.5 percent of the total covered wages in the prior calendar year.

Funding Source

The UTF is funded by employer contributions (payroll taxes) and benefit reimbursements from nonprofit entities and governmental units that are paid in lieu of payroll taxes. The UTF may receive repayable advances from the general fund of the Treasury when it has insufficient balances to make advances to states or to pay the federal share of extended benefits.

The UTF invests its receipts in U.S. government securities and then draws on them when the government needs to pay unemployment benefits and/or cover administrative costs. In addition, the Treasury maintains a trust fund account for each state that it can use to build up reserves in times of economic stability. Forty-nine states have triggers that automatically raise state employer taxes when UTF balances fall below a specific level.

States finance the costs of regular unemployment insurance benefits and their half of the permanent Extended Benefits Program with employer payroll taxes imposed on at least the first $7,000 paid annually to each employee.

Differences between Estimated and Actual Outlays

Based on a 5-year average, estimated outlays from the UTF differed from actual outlays by about $9.4 billion per year, or 29.6 percent, in absolute value terms. However, the actual annual differences varied between an overestimate of about $5 billion and an underestimate of about $22 billion. Table 15 presents the estimated and actual outlays associated with the unemployment program by fiscal year.

Table 15. Estimated and Actual Unemployment Trust Fund Outlays, by Fiscal Year

Nominal dollars in millions			
Fiscal year	**Original outlay estimate**	**Actual outlays**	**Difference**
2000	$25,773	$20,790	$4,983
2001	24,708	27,989	-3,281
2002	28,443	50,841	-22,398
2003	40,795	54,617	-13,822
2004	39,830	42,525	-2,695
5-year average dollar difference			$-7,443
5-year average difference as a percent of average estimated outlays			-23.3%
5-year average dollar difference (absolute value)			$9,436
5-year percentage difference (absolute value)			29.6%

Source: GAO analysis of President's budget data.

Explanation of Key Differences

Because the overall unemployment rate increased over the 5 fiscal years, actual UTF outlays also increased as would be expected. UTF outlays are highly sensitive to changes in the unemployment rate. For example, between 2000 and 2001 the 17.5 percent increase in the unemployment rate was associated with a 34.6 percent increase in actual UTF outlays. This relationship is best illustrated by referring to figure 8.

Between 2001 and 2002, UTF outlays increased 81.6 percent in response to a 23.4 percent increase in the unemployment rate. In 2002, part of the outlay increase was due to legislation extending federally-funded unemployment insurance benefits through the Temporary Employment Compensation Act of 2002 (TEUC) which resulted in unanticipated UTF outlays. The unemployment rate continued to rise during this time as 130,000 workers were displaced after the events on September 11, 2001, and the economic recession persisted. Between 2002 and 2003, TEUC benefits were extended and the unemployment rate continued to increase but did so at a decreasing rate. The 3.4 percent increase in the unemployment rate and the subsequent extension of TEUC led to the 7.4 percent increase in UTF outlays. Between 2003 and 2004, the unemployment rate decreased by 8.3 percent and outlays decreased by about 22 percent. Table 16 presents the Department of Labor's (Labor) explanation for differences between estimated and actual outlays.

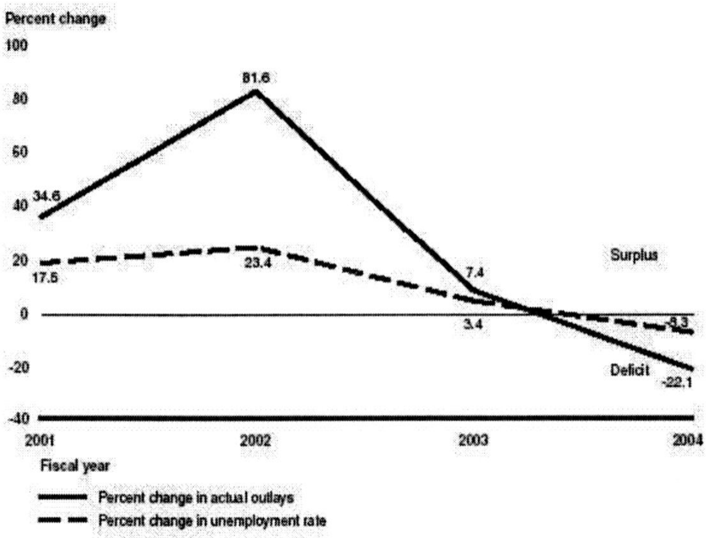

Source: GAO analysis of data from the U.S. Bureau of Labor Statistics and the President's budgets.

Figure 8. Percent Change in Unemployment Rate versus Percent Change in Actual UTF

Illustrative Triggers and Responses

Currently, when funds accumulating in federal unemployment accounts reach statutorily set limits, a distribution of the "excess" funds from the UTF to individual states' accounts in the U.S. Treasury is automatically triggered based on each state's share of covered wages. These distributions are known as "Reed Distributions."[58] Congress can also legislatively trigger a special distribution[59] as it did in March 2002, which provided $8 billion in distributions to all 50 states, the District of Columbia, Puerto Rico, and the Virgin Islands and extended UTF benefits up to an additional 13 weeks longer than the maximum 26 weeks previously allowed by most states.

One potential option to constrain federal spending would be to increase the statutory cap on federal unemployment accounts, thus making it more difficult to trigger Reed Distributions to states. By making it more difficult to trip the trigger, funds could continue to build during economic prosperity and be available to states when truly needed to counter rising unemployment.

A different alternative for constraining growth would be to establish a trigger using a measure of economic prosperity—such as GDP growth in a specified number of consecutive quarters. If this trigger was reached, federal unemployment taxes would automatically increase, allowing trust fund balances to rise. To avoid procyclical effects, these taxes could be automatically reduced again using periods of rising unemployment or recession as the trigger for that action.

Table 16. Explanation of Differences between Estimated and Actual Unemployment Trust Fund Outlays

Nominal dollars in billions			
Fiscal year and dollar differences[a]	**Labor's explanation of differences**		
	Legislative	**Economic**	**Technical**
2000 $5.0		An overestimate of the unemployment rate (5 percent estimated versus 4 percent actual) explained $4.7 billion of the difference.	
2001 $-3.3		An underestimate of the recipiency rate[b] (38 percent estimated versus 42 percent actual) explained $2.9 billion of the difference. The recipiency rate increased from 37 percent the prior year, which is typical for a recession, but was unanticipated.[c]	
2002 $-22.4	TEUC[d] enactment resulted in $7.9 billion of unanticipated outlays.	A 1.1 percent underestimate of the unemployment rate due to recession resulted in a $6.6 billion difference. Underestimates of the recipiency rate and the average weekly benefit accounted for about $4.8 billion and $2.4 billion in outlays, respectively.[e]	

2003 $-13.9	TEUC extension resulted in $11 billion of unanticipated outlays.	An underestimate of the unemployment rate accounted for an additional $2.9 billion.	
2004 $-2.7	TEUC extension resulted in $4.3 billion of unanticipated outlays.	Overestimates of the recipiency rate and average weekly benefit partly offset the TEUC extension.	

Source: Department of Labor.

Notes: Primary drivers of outlay differences are marked in bold.

[a] A negative difference means that actual outlays were higher than originally estimated. A positive difference means that actual outlays were less than originally estimated.

[b] The recipiency rate refers to the number of benefit claims and, more specifically, is the ratio of the insured unemployed (claimants) to the total number of unemployed. The rate tends to vary between 35 and 45 percent.

[c] According to the CRS, the terrorist attacks of September 11, 2001 are directly attributed to displacing 130,000 employees.

[d] The Temporary Extended Unemployment Compensation Act (TEUC), as amended, temporarily extended unemployment benefits from March 2002 through December 2004.

[e] Department of Labor officials did not include the $8 billion Reed Distribution in 2002 as part of the explanation of the difference between estimated and actual outlays in fiscal year 2002 because it was considered an intragovernmental transfer and was not recorded until the states used the money held in the U.S. Treasury. Reed Distributions to states' accounts occur when funds accumulating in federal unemployment accounts reach statutorily set limits.

APPENDIX II: ANALYSIS OF TOTAL OUTLAYS, RECEIPTS, AND FISCAL POSITION

While the focus of this chapter is on budget triggers as they relate to selected case study accounts, we have included our analysis of aggregate receipts, outlays, and surplus/deficit measures to provide broader context. Findings related to our seven case study accounts and the reasons for differences between estimated and actual outlays are discussed in the body of this chapter. More detailed summaries of each account are included in appendix I.

Aggregate Mandatory Spending Estimates Were Close to Actual Outlays but Large Differences Appear at the Account Level

In the aggregate, original estimates of total mandatory spending were fairly close to actual results, however large discrepancies were evident at the account level. During fiscal years 2000 through 2004, estimated total mandatory outlays differed from actuals by no more than about 2 percent, or $24 billion. However at the account level, average estimated and actual outlays varied greatly. While the largest difference was in the Interest on the Public Debt account—a result of other changes—other accounts also showed significant changes between estimated and actual outlays. Alternatively, there are many mandatory accounts with virtually no differences between estimated and actual outlays. The variation among individual accounts was not apparent at the aggregate level because the combination of positive and negative differences offset each other.

Figure 9 shows that total spending on mandatory programs was expected to rise throughout the 5-year period and that resulting outlays were just slightly higher than expected.

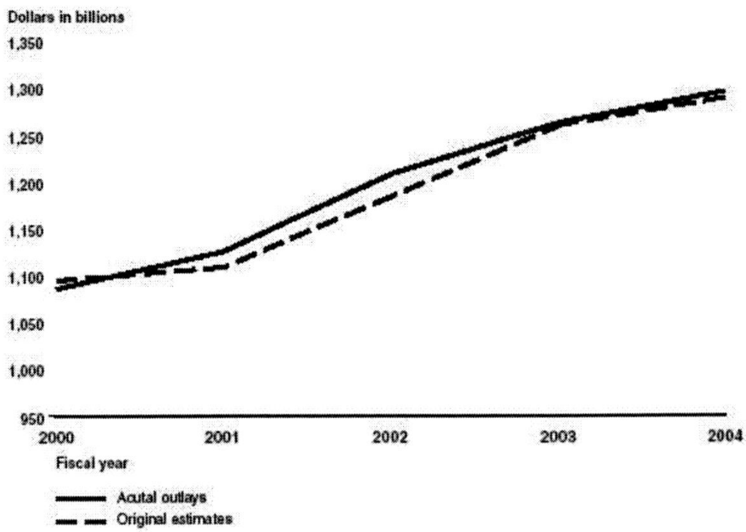

Source: GAO analysis of President's budget data.

Figure 9. Estimated and Actual Total Mandatory Outlays for FYs 2000–2004, constant 2004 dollars

Although aggregate estimates were close to actual estimates, the continued actual and forecasted growth in mandatory programs has raised concerns about the government's long-term fiscal outlook. Addressing growth in mandatory spending is an important but complicated matter that requires looking below the aggregate and into specific programs.

Differences between Estimated and Actual Mandatory Outlays Had Limited Effect on the Unified Deficit/Surplus

The unified budget deficit/surplus measures federal fiscal position, that is, the difference between total annual receipts and outlays. Not surprisingly, the relatively small differences between total estimated and actual mandatory outlays had a limited effect on the unified budget surplus/deficit. In most cases throughout fiscal years 2000 through 2004, the difference between estimated and actual mandatory outlays accounted for approximately 7 percent or less of the difference between the estimated and actual fiscal position. Despite the fact that mandatory outlays were close to expectations, surplus/deficit measures proved difficult to estimate throughout the 5-year period, primarily because of misestimates of federal receipts.[60]

During fiscal years 2000 through 2004, deficit/surplus projections were generally more optimistic than reality. Figure 10 illustrates the estimated and actual fiscal position (surplus/deficit) throughout the 5-year period. Although increasing surpluses were projected for the first three years followed by growing deficits, actual results show that the nation's fiscal position in fact declined throughout the 5-year timeframe. In addition, projections for fiscal years 2003 and 2004 show that the deficit was expected to grow but not to the magnitude that ultimately resulted.

The fiscal position represents the difference between total federal revenues and outlays in a given year. Although mandatory spending constitutes more than half of total federal spending, misestimates of the amount of mandatory spending did not contribute significantly to the differences between the predicted and actual fiscal position. According to the detailed receipt and outlay data shown in table 17, the mandatory outlay difference in most cases accounted for less than 7 percent of the difference between the estimated and actual fiscal position with one exception. In fiscal year 2001, the mandatory outlay estimating error had a larger

Table 17. Aggregate Estimated and Actual Outlays and Receipts for Fiscal Years 2000–2004

Constant 2004 dollars in billions					
	Original estimate	Actual	Difference	Percent of original estimate	Percent of difference
Fiscal Year 2000					
Receipts	$2,055.7	$2,210.9	-$155.3	-7.6%	119.7%
Outlays	1,927.6	1,953.1	-25.5	-1.3	19.7
Discretionary spending	645.7	671.2	-25.4	-3.9	19.6
Mandatory spending	1,093.7	1,085.0	8.6	0.8	-6.6
Offsetting receipts	-46.8	-46.5	-0.3	0.7	0.3
Net interest	234.9	243.3	-8.4	-3.6	6.5
Surplus/Deficit	$128.1	$257.8	-$129.7	-101.3%	100.0%
Fiscal Year 2001					
Receipts	$2,154.1	$2,124.4	$29.7	1.4%	49.9%
Outlays	1,957.8	1,987.7	-29.9	-1.5	-50.1
Discretionary spending	676.3	692.7	-16.4	-2.4	-27.6
Mandatory spending	1,107.6	1,125.1	-17.5	-1.6	-29.4
Offsetting receipts	-48.4	-50.1	1.7	-3.5	2.9
Net interest	222.2	220.0	2.2	1.0	3.8
Surplus/Deficit	$196.3	$136.7	$59.6	30.3%	100.0%
Fiscal Year 2002					
Receipts	$2,296.5	$1,941.7	$354.7	15.4%	87.0%
Outlays	2,054.2	2,107.1	-52.8	-2.6	-13.0
Discretionary spending	724.7	769.4	-44.6	-6.2	-11.0
Mandatory spending	1,184.1	1,208.2	-24.1	-2.0	-5.9
Offsetting receipts	-51.8	-49.7	-2.1	4.0	-0.5
Net interest	197.1	179.1	18.0	9.1	4.4
Surplus/Deficit	$242.2	-$165.3	$407.6	168.3%	100.0%
Fiscal Year 2003					
Receipts	$2,093.5	$1,821.9	$271.6	13.0%	89.3%
Outlays	2,175.4	2,207.8	-32.4	-1.5	-10.7
Discretionary spending	806.5	843.7	-37.2	-4.6	-12.2
Mandatory spending	1,260.0	1,263.2	-3.2	-0.3	-1.0
Offsetting receipts	-75.7	-55.6	-20.1	26.6	-6.6
Net interest	184.7	156.5	28.2	15.3	9.3
Surplus/Deficit	-$81.9	-$386.0	$304.0	-371.0%	100.0%
Receipts	$1,922.0	$1,880.1	$42.0	2.2%	40.1%

Outlays	2,229.4	2,292.2	-62.8	-2.8	-59.9
Discretionary spending	818.8	895.4	-76.6	-9.4	-73.1
Mandatory spending	1,287.9	1,295.1	-7.2	-0.6	-6.9
Offsetting receipts	-53.7	-58.5	4.8	-8.9	4.6
Net interest	176.4	160.2	16.2	9.2	15.5
Surplus/Deficit	-$307.4	-$412.1	$104.7	-34.1%	100.0%

Source: GAO analysis of President's budget data.

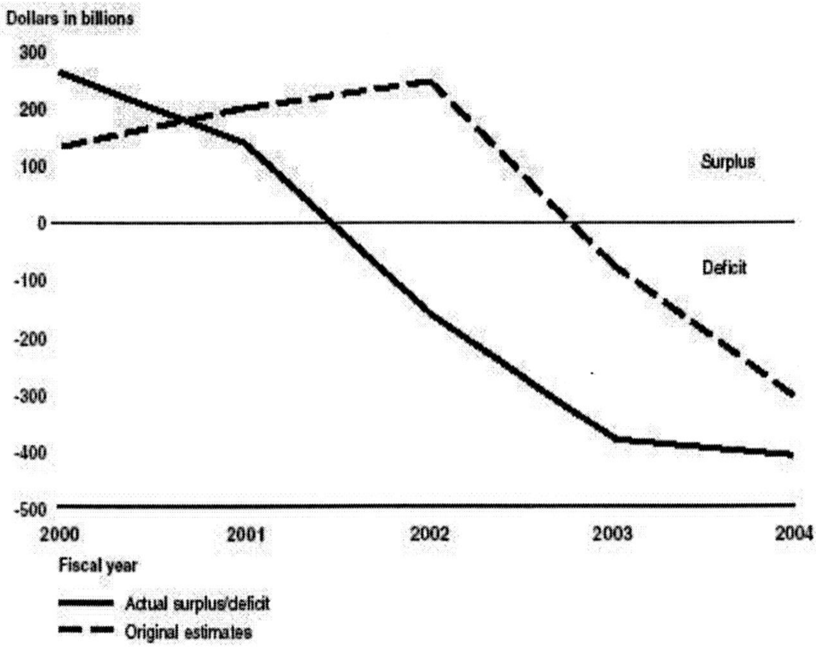

Source: GAO analysis of President's budget data.

Figure 10. Estimated and Actual Surplus/Deficit, Fiscal Years 2000–2004, constant 2004 dollars

than usual effect—approximately 29 percent—on the fiscal position estimating error. While this particular year stands out in the analysis, it is a reasonable result given that the total amount of error in surplus/deficit projections was much smaller—approximately 30 percent or $60 billion—compared with any other year during the 5-year period. For example, a $242 billion surplus was projected for 2002 when in fact the nation's fiscal position changed from surplus to deficit, resulting in a $165 billion deficit for that year.[61] This discrepancy represented a misestimate of approximately 168 percent. In both fiscal years 2001 and 2002, mandatory outlay estimates differed from actual outlays by approximately 2 percent. This relatively small difference accounted for over one quarter of the resulting error in the surplus projection for 2001 because the difference between estimated and actual receipts also was relatively small. It accounted for less than one-tenth of the total error in the fiscal position projection for 2002 because the difference between estimated and actual receipts was much larger. Effects similar to the latter occurred more frequently throughout the 5-year period, indicating that estimation errors in mandatory outlays had a limited effect on fiscal position.

In contrast, revenue estimate inaccuracies proved to have a greater effect on projections of the nation's fiscal position. Throughout the 5-year period, total estimated outlays differed from actual outlays by no more than 3 percent while total estimated receipts differed from actual receipts by up to 15 percent in absolute value terms. This suggests that revenue, rather than outlay estimates, led most significantly to the discrepancies in surplus/deficit projections. Figure 11 shows the total estimated and actual federal receipts in dollar terms for each year we reviewed.[62]

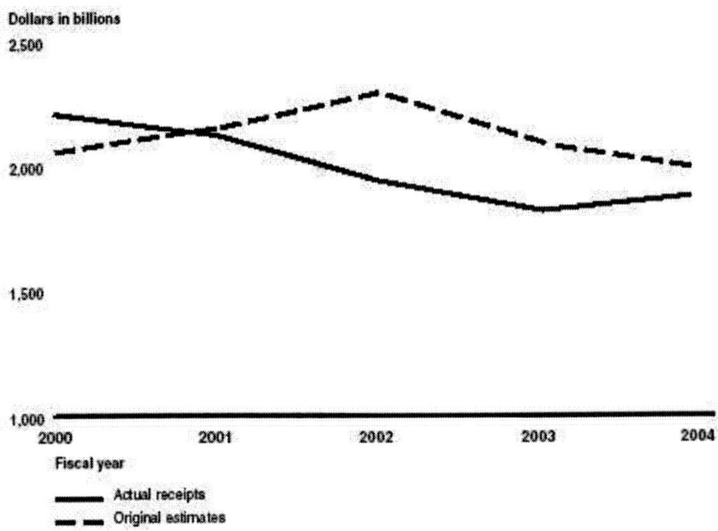

Source: GAO analysis of President's budget data.

Figure 11. Total Estimated and Actual Receipts, Fiscal Years 2000–2004, constant 2004 dollars

As mentioned earlier in this chapter, the greatest revenue estimating errors occurred in 2000, 2002, and 2003, which correlate with the years in which the fiscal position projections were the most inaccurate. For example, in fiscal year 2002, an approximate 2.6 percent underestimate in total outlays coupled with an approximate 15.4 percent overestimate of receipts translated into a large shift in fiscal position from surplus to deficit. Similar effects occurred in 2000 and 2003. As shown in table 18, the driving source of revenue misestimates in any given year varied, but individual and corporate income taxes often proved difficult to estimate.

Table 18. Revenue Estimates and Actual Results by Source and Fiscal Year

Constant 2004 dollars in millions				
Component of revenue	**Original estimate**	**Actual**	**Actual minus original**	**Percent of original**
Fiscal Year 2000				
Individual income taxes	$982,250	$1,096,574	-$114,324	-11.6%
Corporate income taxes	206,721	226,298	-19,578	-9.5
Social insurance taxes and contributions	694,901	712,721	-17,820	-2.6
Excise taxes	76,312	75,180	1,132	1.5
Estate and gift taxes	29,445	31,670	-2,225	-7.6
Customs duties	20,048	21,740	-1,692	-8.4
Miscellaneous receipts	45,991	46,753	-762	-1.7
Total	**$2,055,668**	**$2,210,937**	**-$155,269**	**-7.6%**
Fiscal Year 2001				
Individual income taxes	$1,037,459	$1,060,855	-$23,396	-2.3%
Corporate income taxes	207,799	161,181	46,618	22.4
Social insurance taxes and contributions	727,707	740,389	-12,682	-1.7
Excise taxes	81,805	70,663	11,143	13.6
Estate and gift taxes	34,465	30,300	4,165	12.1
Customs duties	22,267	20,665	1,602	7.2
Miscellaneous receipts	42,590	40,341	2,249	5.3
Total	**$2,154,093**	**$2,124,393**	**$29,699**	**1.4%**
Fiscal Year 2002				
Individual income taxes	$1,130,332	$899,356	$230,977	20.4%
Corporate income taxes	229,239	155,117	74,122	32.3

Table 18. (Continued)

Constant 2004 dollars in millions				
Component of revenue	**Original estimate**	**Actual**	**Actual minus original**	**Percent of original**
Social insurance taxes and contributions	760,476	734,241	26,234	3.4
Excise taxes	77,557	70,190	7,367	9.5
Estate and gift taxes	30,070	27,773	2,297	7.6
Customs duties	23,614	19,491	4,123	17.5
Miscellaneous receipts	45,165	35,547	9,618	21.3
Total	**$2,296,452**	**$1,941,715**	**$354,737**	**15.4%**
Fiscal Year 2003				
Individual income taxes	$1,028,676	$811,304	$217,372	21.1%
Corporate income taxes	210,047	134,701	75,346	35.9
Social insurance taxes and contributions	765,831	728,793	37,038	4.8
Excise taxes	70,552	69,022	1,530	2.2
Estate and gift taxes	23,509	22,446	1,063	4.5
Customs duties	20,244	20,303	-58	-0.3
Miscellaneous receipts	-25,371	35,308	-60,679	239.2
Total	**$2,093,489**	**$1,821,877**	**$271,612**	**13.0%**
Fiscal Year 2004				
Individual income taxes	$849,880	$808,959	$40,921	4.8%
Corporate income taxes	169,060	189,371	-20,311	-12.0
Social insurance taxes and contributions	764,548	733,407	31,141	4.1
Excise taxes	70,905	69,855	1,050	1.5
Estate and gift taxes	23,379	24,831	-1,452	-6.2
Customs duties	20,713	21,083	-370	-1.8
Miscellaneous receipts	38,540	32,565	5,975	15.5
Total	**$1,937,025**	**$1,880,071**	**$56,954**	**2.9%**

Source: GAO analysis of President's budget data.

APPENDIX III MANDATORY BUDGET ACCOUNTS

Table 19. Budget Accounts with Greater than 50 percent Mandatory Outlays

Dollars in millions			
Obs. #	Agency	Account	5-year avg. dollar change (absolute value)
1	Treasury	Interest on Treasury debt securities (gross)	$20,016
2	Veterans Affairs	Disability compensation benefits*	9,977
3	Labor	Unemployment trust fund	9,436
4	Veterans Affairs	Compensation*	7,423
5	Agriculture	Commodity Credit Corporation fund	6,944
6	Health and Human Services	Federal supplementary medical insurance trust fund	6,427
7	Health and Human Services	Federal hospital insurance trust fund	5,622
8	Office of Personnel Management	Employees health benefits fund*	5,065
9	Health and Human Services	Grants to States for Medicaid	4,220
10	Railroad Retirement Board	Rail industry pension fund	4,077
11	Health and Human Services	Payments to health care trust funds	3,800
12	Housing and Urban Development	FHA—mutual mortgage insurance program account*	2,892
13	Veterans Affairs	Pensions benefits*	2,528
14	Education	Federal direct student loan program account	2,370
15	Health and Human Services	Immediate helping hand prescription drug plan*	2,240
16	Postal Service	Postal Service fund	2,129
17	Housing and Urban Development	FHA—mutual mortgage and cooperative housing insurance funds liquidating account	2,067
18	Agriculture	Food stamp program	2,058
19	Treasury	Temporary State fiscal assistance fund*	2,000
20	Social Security Administration	Federal old-age and survivors insurance trust fund	1,979
21	Office of Personnel Management	Payment to civil service retirement and disability fund	1,862
22	Allowances	Bipartisan economic security plan*	1,600
23	Treasury	Payment where child credit exceeds liability for tax	1,582
24	Education	Federal family education loan program account	1,573
25	Federal Communications Commission	Universal service fund	1,539
26	Health and Human Services	Temporary assistance for needy families	1,322
27	Health and Human Services	Allowance for Medicare modernization*	1,200

Table 19. (Continued)

Dollars in millions			
Obs. #	**Agency**	**Account**	**5-year avg. dollar change (absolute value)**
28	Justice	September 11th victim compensation (general fund)*	1,192
29	Social Security Administration	Payments to social security trust funds	1,168
30	Labor	Advances to the Unemployment trust fund and other* funds	1,154
31	Treasury	Refunding internal revenue collections, interest	1,153
32	Office of Personnel Management	Government payment for annuitants, employees health benefits	1,081
33	Treasury	Payment where earned income credit exceeds liability for tax	1,004
34	Office of Personnel Management	Civil service retirement and disability fund	988
35	Labor	Black lung disability trust fund	987
36	Housing and Urban Development	FHA—general and special risk insurance funds liquidating account	964
37	Health and Human Services	State children's health insurance fund	922
38	Transportation	Compensation for air carriers*	910
39	Social Security Administration	Federal disability insurance trust fund	865
40	International Assistance Programs	Foreign military sales trust fund	850
41	Federal Deposit Insurance Corporation	Bank insurance fund*	844
42	Treasury	Payment to the Resolution Funding Corporation	799
43	International Assistance Programs	United States quota, International Monetary Fund*	793
44	Federal Communications Commission	Spectrum auction program account*	785
45	Education	Federal family education loan liquidating account	778
46	Office of Personnel Management	Employees and retired employees health benefits funds*	775
47	Social Security Administration	Supplemental security income program	759
48	Agriculture	Rural electrification and telecommunications liquidating account	681
49	Justice	Immigration support*	652
50	Small Business Administration	Business loan program account*	625
51	Treasury	Interest paid to credit financing accounts	625

Table 19. (Continued)

Dollars in millions			
Obs. #	Agency	Account	5-year avg. dollar change (absolute value)
52	Justice	Crime victims fund	609
53	Veterans Affairs	Housing program account	594
54	Labor	Pension benefit guaranty corporation fund	581
55	Treasury	Claims, judgments, and relief acts	569
56	Agriculture	Commodity Credit Corporation export loans program account	553
57	Housing and Urban Development	FHA—mutual mortgage insurance capital reserve account*	543
58	Housing and Urban Development	FHA-general and special risk program account*	536
59	Export-Import Bank of the United States	Export-Import Bank loans program account*	516
60	Health and Human Services	Child care entitlement to States	499
61	Treasury	Federal Financing Bank	488
62	Homeland Security	Citizenship and Immigration Services*	471
63	Agriculture	Agricultural credit insurance fund program account*	467
64	Treasury	Exchange stabilization fund	440
65	Justice	Immigration services*	418
66	Labor	Reemployment accounts*	400
67	Health and Human Services	Payments to States for foster care and adoption assistance	392
68	Other Defense Civil Programs	Payment to Department of Defense Medicare-eligible retiree health care fund*	390
69	Other Defense Civil Programs	Payment to military retirement fund	376
70	Railroad Retirement Board	National railroad retirement investment trust*	367
71	Railroad Retirement Board	Railroad social security equivalent benefit account	363
72	Other Defense Civil Programs	Department of Defense Medicare-Eligible retiree health care fund*	361
73	Labor	Welfare to work jobs	353
74	Homeland Security	Retired Pay*	352
75	Department of Defense—Military	Allied contributions and cooperation account	346
76	Veterans Affairs	Education benefits	324
77	Tennessee Valley Authority	Tennessee Valley Authority fund	323
78	Small Business Administration	Disaster loans program account*	319
79	Energy	Bonneville Power Administration fund	317

Table 19. (Continued)

Obs. #	Agency	Account	5-year avg. dollar change (absolute value)
Dollars in millions			
80	Department of Defense—Military	Pentagon reservation maintenance revolving fund*	317
81	Other Defense Civil Programs	Military retirement fund	312
82	Department of Defense—Military	Iraq relief and reconstruction fund, Army*	310
83	Agriculture	Federal crop insurance corporation fund	310
84	Labor	Payments to the Unemployment trust fund*	305
85	Federal Deposit Insurance Corporation	Savings association insurance fund*	295
86	Health and Human Services	Payments to States for child support enforcement and family support programs	284
87	Interior	Mineral leasing and associated payments	279
88	Treasury	Air transportation stabilization program account*	273
89	Homeland Security	National Flood Insurance Fund*	269
90	Interior	Interior Franchise Fund*	260
91	Agriculture	Farm security and rural investment programs*	254
92	Agriculture	Funds for strengthening markets, income, and supply (section 32)	241
93	Health and Human Services	Allowance for transitional Medicare low-income drug assistance*	240
94	Federal Emergency Management Agency	National flood insurance fund*	227
95	Housing and Urban Development	Guarantees of mortgage-backed securities liquidating account*	223
96	Veterans Affairs	Vocational rehabilitation and employment benefits*	202
97	Department of Defense—Military	National defense stockpile transaction fund*	197
98	National Credit Union Administration	Credit union share insurance fund	195
99	Federal Deposit Insurance Corporation	FSLIC resolution fund	189
100	Export-Import Bank of the United States	Export-Import Bank of the United States liquidating account	188
101	Office of Personnel Management	Employees life insurance fund	187

Table 19. (Continued)

Dollars in millions			
Obs. #	**Agency**	**Account**	**5-year avg. dollar change (absolute value)**
102	Education	Federal student loan reserve fund*	182
103	Agriculture	Rural electrification and telecommunications loans program account*	180
104	Transportation	Coast Guard military retirement fund*	178
105	Agriculture	Child nutrition programs	177
106	Health and Human Services	Social services block grant	177
107	Treasury	Payment where health care credit exceeds liability for tax*	177
108	Transportation	Retired pay*	174
109	Agriculture	Rural development insurance fund liquidating account	174
110	Labor	Energy employees occupational illness compensation fund*	160
111	Labor	Federal unemployment benefits and allowances	159
112	Veterans Affairs	Supply fund*	159
113	Health and Human Services	Ricky Ray hemophilia relief fund*	150
114	Transportation	Payment to Coast Guard military retirement fund*	147
115	Social Security Administration	Payment to social security trust funds post-1956 military service wage credits*	146
116	Agriculture	Forest Service trust funds	139
117	Agriculture	Rural housing insurance fund liquidating account	131
118	Treasury	Restitution of forgone interest*	129
119	International Assistance Programs	Economic assistance loans liquidating account	127
120	Agriculture	Agricultural credit insurance fund liquidating account	125
121	Interior	Tribal special fund	123
122	Interior	Working capital fund*	118
123	Housing and Urban Development	Housing for the elderly or handicapped fund liquidating account	118
124	District of Columbia	Federal payment to the District of Columbia pension fund	117
125	Agriculture	Forest Service permanent appropriations	116
126	Small Business Administration	Disaster loan fund liquidating account	116
127	Health and Human Services	Payment to the Ricky Ray hemophilia relief fund*	116
128	Farm Credit System Financial Assistance	Financial Assistance Corporation assistance fund	116
	Corporation	liquidating account	
129	Transportation	Ocean freight differential	115

Table 19. (Continued)

Dollars in millions			
Obs. #	Agency	Account	5-year avg. dollar change (absolute value)
130	Legislative Branch	Payments to copyright owners	113
131	Veterans Affairs	Housing liquidating account	104
132	Treasury	Contribution for annuity benefits*	103
133	Social Security Administration	Special benefits for disabled coal miners*	95
134	Labor	Special benefits for disabled coal miners*	94
135	International Assistance Programs	Foreign military loan liquidating account	93
136	Treasury	Treasury forfeiture fund*	88
137	Small Business Administration	Business loan fund liquidating account	87
138	Labor	Special benefits	86
139	International Assistance Programs	Overseas Private Investment Corporation program account*	86
140	Interior	Miscellaneous permanent payment accounts	82
141	Agriculture	Commodity Credit Corporation guaranteed loans liquidating account	81
142	Treasury	Payment of anti-terrorism judgments*	80
143	Judicial Branch	Judiciary filing fees	80
144	Education	Rehabilitation services and disability research	79
145	Treasury	Payment where alternative to failing school credit exceeds liability for tax*	76
146	International Assistance Programs	Foreign military financing loan program account*	70
147	Veterans Affairs	National service life insurance fund	70
148	Treasury	Internal revenue collections for Puerto Rico	68
149	Corps of Engineers—Civil Works	Rivers and harbors contributed funds	67
150	Health and Human Services	Retirement pay and medical benefits for commissioned officers	67
151	Transportation	Miscellaneous trust funds	65
152	United Mine Workers of America Benefit Funds	United Mine Workers of America combined benefit fund	63
153	Agriculture	Healthy investments in rural environments*	63
154	Railroad Retirement Board	Federal payments to the railroad retirement accounts	61
155	Transportation	Maritime guaranteed loan (Title XI) program account*	60
156	Agriculture	Rural telephone bank liquidating account	60

Table 19. (Continued)

Dollars in millions			
Obs. #	**Agency**	**Account**	**5-year avg. dollar change (absolute value)**
157	General Services Administration	General supply fund*	60
158	Veterans Affairs	Burial benefits*	59
159	Treasury	Continued dumping and subsidy offset*	56
160	Transportation	Aviation insurance revolving fund*	56
161	Agriculture	Fund for rural America	55
162	Agriculture	Payments to states stabilization*	54
163	Health and Human Services	Program management*	52
164	Veterans Affairs	Burial benefits and miscellaneous assistance*	51
165	Treasury	Refunds, transfers, and expenses of operation, Puerto Rico*	51
166	Federal Communications Commission	Pioneer's preference settlement*	50
167	Treasury	Restoration of lost interest, Medicare trust funds*	49
168	Corps of Engineers—Civil Works	Revolving fund*	48
169	Agriculture	Expenses, Public Law 480, foreign assistance programs, Agriculture liquidating account	48
170	Agriculture	Expenses and refunds, inspection and grading of farm products*	48
171	Justice	Working capital fund*	48
172	Department of Defense—Military	Army conventional ammunition working capital fund*	48
173	United States Enrichment Corporation Fund	United States Enrichment Corporation Fund*	47
174	Health and Human Services	Public Health Service Commissioned Corps retirement fund*	47
175	Department of Defense—Military	Surcharge collections, sales of commissary stores, Defense*	46
176	Interior	Recreation fee permanent appropriations	45
177	Housing and Urban Development	Working capital fund*	44
178	Health and Human Services	Transitional drug assistance, Federal supplementary medical insurance trust fund*	43
179	Treasury	Confiscated and vested Iraqi property and assets*	42
180	Labor	Administrative expenses, Energy employees occupational illness compensation fund*	40
181	Interior	Lower Colorado River Basin development fund	40

Table 19. (Continued)

Dollars in millions			
Obs. #	**Agency**	**Account**	**5-year avg. dollar change (absolute value)**
182	Treasury	Federal Reserve Bank reimbursement fund	38
183	Legislative Branch	Government Printing Office revolving fund	38
184	Justice	Public safety officers' benefits*	37
185	Interior	Permanent operating funds	37
186	Department of State	Working capital fund*	36
187	Treasury	Financial agent services*	36
188	Commerce	Census working capital fund*	36
189	Justice	Federal Prison Industries, Incorporated*	36
190	Federal Deposit Insurance Corporation	Federal deposit insurance fund*	36
191	Interior	Upper Colorado River Basin fund*	35
192	Farm Credit System Insurance Corporation	Farm credit system insurance fund	35
193	Health and Human Services	Payment to health care trust funds for post-1956 military service wage credits*	35
194	Justice	Assets forfeiture fund	35
195	Health and Human Services	Health care fraud and abuse control account	34
196	Health and Human Services	Health education assistance loans program account*	33
197	International Assistance Programs	Housing and other credit guaranty programs liquidating account	33
198	Agriculture	Initiative for future agriculture and food systems*	33
199	Justice	Radiation exposure compensation trust fund*	32
200	Homeland Security	Boat Safety*	30
201	Agriculture	Payments to States, northern spotted owl guarantee, Forest	29
202	Treasury	Working capital fund*	29
203	Corps of Engineers—Civil Works	Coastal wetlands restoration trust fund	29
204	Transportation	Boat safety*	28
205	Other Defense Civil Programs	Contributions*	28
206	Homeland Security	Oil Spill Recovery*	28
207	Transportation	Oil spill recovery*	28
208	Interior	Tribal trust fund	27
209	Interior	Compact of free association	27
210	Commerce	Promote and develop fishery products and research pertaining to American fisheries	26

Table 19. (Continued)

Dollars in millions			
Obs. #	**Agency**	**Account**	**5-year avg. dollar change (absolute value)**
211	Health and Human Services	Payment to Public Health Service Commissioned Corps retirement system*	26
212	Central Intelligence Agency	Payment to Central Intelligence Agency retirement and disability system fund	26
213	Housing and Urban Development	Low-rent public housing—loans and other expenses	25
214	Environmental Protection Agency	Re-registration and expedited processing revolving fund*	24
215	Health and Human Services	HHS service and supply fund*	23
216	Interior	Abandoned mine reclamation fund*	23
217	Federal Emergency Management Agency	Disaster assistance direct loan program account*	23
218	Justice	Fees and expenses of witnesses	23
219	Judicial Branch	Judiciary information technology fund	22
220	Health and Human Services	Vaccine injury compensation program trust fund	22
221	Interior	Natural resource damage assessment fund	22
222	Agriculture	Miscellaneous trust funds*	21
223	Health and Human Services	Promoting safe and stable families	21
224	Interior	Payments to the United States territories, fiscal assistance	21
225	Agriculture	McGovern-Dole international food for education and child nutrition program*	20
226	Treasury	Assessment funds	20
227	Transportation	Essential air service and rural airport improvement fund*	20
228	Housing and Urban Development	Revolving fund (liquidating programs)*	18
229	Agriculture	Perishable Agricultural Commodities Act fund	18
230	International Assistance Programs	Urban and environmental credit program account*	18
231	Justice	Commissary funds, Federal prisons (trust revolving fund)*	18
232	Veterans Affairs	Veterans special life insurance fund	18
233	Agriculture	Working capital fund*	17
234	Federal Emergency Management Agency	Flood map modernization fund*	17
235	Agriculture	Trade adjustment assistance for farmers*	16
236	Interior	Federal aid in wildlife restoration	16
237	Homeland Security	Refunds, transfers, and expenses of operation, Puerto Rico*	16

Table 19. (Continued)

Dollars in millions			
Obs. #	Agency	Account	5-year avg. dollar change (absolute value)
238	Agriculture	Milk market orders assessment fund*	16
239	Health and Human Services	Health education assistance loans liquidating account	15
240	Transportation	Right-of-way revolving fund liquidating account	15
241	Justice	Payment to radiation exposure compensation trust fund*	15
242	Interior	Working capital fund	15
243	Railroad Retirement Board	Railroad unemployment insurance trust fund	15
244	Department of Defense—Military	Other DOD trust funds	14
245	Veterans Affairs	Franchise fund*	14
246	Treasury	Office of Thrift Supervision*	14
247	Justice	Diversion control fee account	14
248	General Services Administration	Panama Canal revolving fund*	14
249	National Science Foundation	Donations	13
250	Farm Credit System Financial Assistance Corporation	Financial assistance corporation trust fund*	13
251	District of Columbia	District of Columbia Federal pension liability trust fund	12
252	Interior	Colorado River dam fund, Boulder Canyon project	12
253	Interior	Sport fish restoration	12
254	Treasury	Presidential election campaign fund*	12
255	United Mine Workers of America Benefit Funds	United Mine Workers of America 1992 benefit plan	12
256	Department of State	Payment to Foreign Service retirement and disability fund	12
257	Health and Human Services	Miscellaneous trust funds	11
258	Commerce	Emergency steel guaranteed loan program account*	11
259	Health and Human Services	State grants and demonstrations*	11
260	Health and Human Services	Children's research and technical assistance	10
261	Agriculture	Rural strategic investment program grants*	10
262	Health and Human Services	Contingency fund*	10
263	Federal Emergency Management Agency	National flood mitigation fund*	10
264	Agriculture	Rural economic development grants	10
265	Interior	Everglades watershed protection*	10

Table 19. (Continued)

Dollars in millions			
Obs. #	**Agency**	**Account**	**5-year avg. dollar change (absolute value)**
266	Interior	Other permanent appropriations	10
267	Health and Human Services	Vaccine injury compensation*	9
268	Federal Emergency Management Agency	Disaster assistance direct loan liquidating account*	9
269	Interior	Interior Franchise Fund*	9
270	Federal Deposit Insurance Corporation	Office of Inspector General	9
271	Veterans Affairs	Post-Vietnam era veterans education account	9
272	Federal Retirement Thrift Investment Board	Program expenses	9
273	Interior	Assistance to territories*	9
274	Commerce	Working capital fund*	8
275	Department of Defense—Military	Buildings maintenance fund*	8
276	Department of State	Miscellaneous trust funds	8
277	Interior	Helium fund	8
278	Other Defense Civil Programs	Education benefits fund	8
279	Justice	Independent counsel	8
280	Corps of Engineers—Civil Works	Washington aqueduct*	8
281	Interior	Reclamation trust funds*	8
282	Agriculture	Rural cooperative development grants*	8
283	Energy	Emergency fund, Western Area Power Administration*	8
284	United Mine Workers of America Benefit Funds	Federal payment to United Mine Workers of America combined benefit fund*	8
285	Agriculture	Rural business investment program account*	7
286	Education	College housing and academic facilities loans liquidating account	7
287	Interior	Miscellaneous trust funds*	7
288	Veterans Affairs	Service-disabled veterans insurance fund	7
289	Legislative Branch	Gift and trust fund accounts	7
290	Agriculture	Local television loan guarantee program account*	7
291	Housing and Urban Development	Community development loan guarantees liquidating account*	7
292	Transportation	Working Capital Fund*	7
293	Department of State	Foreign Service retirement and disability fund	7

Table 19. (Continued)

Dollars in millions

Obs. #	Agency	Account	5-year avg. dollar change (absolute value)
294	Public Company Accounting Oversight Board	Public Company Accounting Oversight Board*	7
295	Agriculture	Miscellaneous trust funds	7
296	Department of Defense—Military	Foreign national employees separation pay	7
297	Transportation	Federal ship financing fund liquidating account	7
298	Interior	Cooperative fund (Papago)*	6
299	Commerce	Coastal zone management fund	6
300	Energy	Continuing fund, Southeastern Power Administration*	6
301	International Assistance Programs	Overseas Private Investment Corporation liquidating account*	6
302	Housing and Urban Development	Rental housing assistance fund*	6
303	Interior	Miscellaneous trust funds	6
304	Treasury	Federal interest liabilities to States	6
305	Department of Defense—Military	Voluntary separation incentive fund	5
306	Labor	Special workers' compensation expenses	5
307	Health and Human Services	State grants and demonstrations*	5
308	Housing and Urban Development	Community development loan guarantees program account*	5
309	Interior	Miscellaneous permanent appropriations	5
310	Interior	Contribution for annuity benefits*	5
311	Health and Human Services	Job opportunities and basic skills training program*	5
312	Veterans Affairs	Miscellaneous veterans housing loans program account*	5
313	Agriculture	Miscellaneous contributed funds*	5
314	Commerce	Economic development revolving fund liquidating account*	5
315	Commerce	Environmental improvement and restoration fund*	5
316	Veterans Affairs	Veterans reopened insurance fund	5
317	Agriculture	Conservation reserve program*	4
318	Veterans Affairs	Canteen service revolving fund*	4
319	Legislative Branch	U.S. Capitol Preservation Commission*	4
320	Commerce	Federal ship financing fund fishing vessels liquidating account*	4
321	Interior	Payments for trust accounting deficiencies*	4

Table 19. (Continued)

Dollars in millions			
Obs. #	**Agency**	**Account**	**5-year avg. dollar change (absolute value)**
322	National Credit Union Administration	Operating fund*	4
323	Railroad Retirement Board	Supplemental annuity pension fund*	4
324	Agriculture	National Sheep Industry Improvement Center*	4
325	Agriculture	Road and trail fund*	4
326	Commerce	Payments to NOAA commissioned officer corps retirement fund*	4
327	Treasury	Administering the public debt*	4
328	International Assistance Programs	Loan guarantees to Israel program account*	4
329	Agriculture	Renewable energy program account*	4
330	District of Columbia	Federal payment for water and sewer services*	4
331	Department of Defense—Military	Host nation support fund for relocation	4
332	Standard Setting Body	Payment to standard setting body*	4
333	Agriculture	Miscellaneous contributed funds	3
334	Interior	Bureau of Reclamation loan liquidating account	3
335	General Services Administration	Disposal of surplus real and related personal property	3
336	Legislative Branch	Gifts and donations	3
337	Commerce	National Oceanic and Atmospheric Administration Commissioned Officer Corps retirement*	3
338	Treasury	Informant payments*	3
339	Legislative Branch	Judiciary office building development and operations fund*	3
340	Department of State	Foreign Service national separation liability trust fund	3
341	Treasury	Refunds, transfers and expenses, Unclaimed and abandoned goods*	3
342	Agriculture	Wetlands reserve program	3
343	Agriculture	Expenses and refunds, inspection and grading of farm products	3
344	Transportation	Operations and maintenance (Harbor services fee collections)*	3
345	Veterans Affairs	General post fund, national homes	3
346	Judicial Branch	Judicial officers' retirement fund	3
347	National Archives and Records Administration	National archives gift fund*	3

Table 19. (Continued)

Dollars in millions			
Obs. #	Agency	Account	5-year avg. dollar change (absolute value)
348	Office of Personnel Management	Government payment for annuitants, employee life insurance	3
349	Vietnam Education Foundation	Vietnam debt repayment fund*	3
350	Agriculture	Miscellaneous contributed funds	2
351	Commerce	Damage assessment and restoration revolving fund	2
352	Housing and Urban Development	Manufactured home inspection and monitoring*	2
353	Interior	Migratory bird conservation account	2
354	Interior	Indian direct loan program account*	2
355	Transportation	Operations and maintenance*	2
356	General Services Administration	Expenses of transportation audit contracts and contract administration	2
357	International Assistance Programs	Miscellaneous trust funds, AID*	2
358	Commerce	Fisheries finance program account*	2
359	Department of Defense—Military	Other DOD trust revolving funds*	2
360	Health and Human Services	Medical facilities guarantee and loan fund	2
361	Veterans Affairs	Service members' group life insurance fund*	2
362	Farm Credit Administration	Revolving fund for administrative expenses*	2
363	Federal Housing Finance Board	Federal housing finance board*	2
364	Judicial Branch	Registry Administration	2
365	Legislative Branch	Compensation of members and related administrative expenses	2
366	Small Business Administration	Pollution control equipment fund liquidating account*	2
367	Corps of Engineers—Civil Works	Permanent appropriations	2
368	Corps of Engineers—Civil Works	Payment to South Dakota terrestrial wildlife habitat restoration trust fund*	2
369	Commerce	Limited access system administration fund*	2
370	Homeland Security	US Customs Refunds, Transfers and Expenses, Unclaimed and Abandoned Goods*	2
371	Agriculture	Wildlife habitat incentives program	2
372	Veterans Affairs	Insurance benefits	2

Table 19. (Continued)

Dollars in millions			
Obs. #	Agency	Account	5-year avg. dollar change (absolute value)
373	District of Columbia	Federal payment to the District of Columbia judicial retirement and survivors annuity fund*	2
374	Morris K. Udall Scholarship and Excellence in National Enviro-nmental Policy Foundation	Environmental dispute resolution fund*	2
375	Agriculture	Farm storage facility loans program account*	2
376	Department of Defense—Military	Miscellaneous special funds*	2
377	Housing and Urban Development	Elderly vouchers*	2
378	Department of State	International litigation fund	2
379	Interior	National Indian Gaming Commission, Gaming activity fees	2
380	Treasury	Interest on uninvested funds	2
381	Transportation	Railroad rehabilitation and improvement liquidating account	2
382	Environmental Protection Agency	Abatement, control, and compliance direct loan liquidating account*	2
383	Panama Canal Commission	Panama Canal Commission dissolution fund*	2
384	Interior	White Earth settlement fund	1
385	Interior	Indian loan guaranty and insurance fund liquidating account*	1
386	Transportation	Emergency preparedness grants	1
387	Legislative Branch	Congressional use of foreign currency, House of Representatives	1
388	Agriculture	Rural communication development fund liquidating account*	1
389	Commerce	Franchise fund*	1
390	Justice	United States trustee system fund*	1
391	Interior	Revolving fund for loans liquidating account	1
392	Interior	National forests fund, Payment to States	1
393	Interior	Recreational fee program	1
394	Interior	Miscellaneous trust funds	1
395	Treasury	Federal tax lien revolving fund*	1
396	International Assistance Programs	Microenterprise and small enterprise development program account*	1
397	Interior	Contributed funds	1

Table 19. (Continued)

Dollars in millions			
Obs. #	Agency	Account	5-year avg. dollar change (absolute value)
398	Interior	Miscellaneous permanent appropriations	1
399	Treasury	Check forgery insurance fund	1
400	Treasury	Payment to terrestrial wildlife habitat restoration trust fund*	1
401	District of Columbia	District of Columbia judicial retirement and survivors annuity fund	1
402	Environmental Protection Agency	Abatement, control, and compliance loan program account*	1
403	Harry S. Truman Scholarship Foundation	Harry S. Truman memorial scholarship trust fund	1
404	James Madison Memorial Fellowship Foundation	James Madison Memorial Fellowship trust fund	1
405	Legislative Branch	John C. Stennis Center for Public Service Training and Development trust fund	1
406	National Archives and Records Administration	National archives trust fund*	1
407	Agriculture	Agricultural resource conservation demonstration program account*	1
408	Agriculture	Rural economic development loans program account*	1
409	Housing and Urban Development	Manufactured housing fees trust fund*	1
410	Labor	Panama Canal Commission compensation fund	1
411	Department of State	Miscellaneous trust funds, information and exchange programs*	1
412	Interior	Operation and maintenance of quarters	1
413	Veterans Affairs	Special therapeutic and rehabilitation activities fund*	1
414	Equal Employment Opportunity Commission	EEOC education, technical assistance, and training revolving fund*	1
415	International Assistance Programs	Peace Corps miscellaneous trust fund	1
416	Judicial Branch	Judicial survivors' annuities fund	1
417	Legislative Branch	Congressional use of foreign currency, Senate	1
418	Social Security Administration	Special benefits for certain World War II veterans*	1
419	Appalachian Regional Commission	Miscellaneous trust funds	1

Table 19. (Continued)

Dollars in millions			
Obs. #	**Agency**	**Account**	**5-year avg. dollar change (absolute value)**
420	Broadcasting Board of Governors	Foreign Service national separation liability trust fund*	1
421	Christopher Columbus Fellowship Foundation	Christopher Columbus Fellowship Foundation*	1
422	Agriculture	Limitation on inspection and weighing services expenses*	1
423	Agriculture	Rural development loan fund liquidating account	1
424	Agriculture	Biomass research and development*	1
425	Energy	Payments to States under Federal Power Act	1
426	Health and Human Services	Revolving fund for certification and other services*	1
427	Labor	Working capital fund*	1
428	Interior	Range improvements	1
429	Interior	Cooperative endangered species conservation fund*	1
430	Interior	Everglades restoration account	1
431	Interior	Leases of lands acquired for flood control, navigation, and allied purposes	1
432	Interior	Contributed funds*	1
433	Treasury	Payment of Government losses in shipment*	1
434	Treasury	Terrorism insurance program*	1
435	Transportation	Amtrak corridor improvement loans liquidating account*	1
436	Federal Emergency Management Agency	National insurance development fund*	1
437	International Assistance Programs	Property management fund*	1
438	International Assistance Programs	Foreign Service national separation liability trust fund	1
439	Judicial Branch	Gifts and donations, Federal Judicial Center Foundation	1
440	Legislative Branch	Senate revolving funds*	1
441	Morris K. Udall Scholarship and Excellence in National Environ-mental Policy Foundation	Morris K. Udall Scholarship and Excellence in National Environmental Policy Foundation*	1
442	Other Defense Civil Programs	White House commission on the national moment of remembrance*	1

Table 19. (Continued)

Dollars in millions

Obs. #	Agency	Account	5-year avg. dollar change (absolute value)
443	Telecommunications Development Fund	Telecommunications development fund*	1
444	Agriculture	Distance learning, telemedicine, and broadband program*	0
445	Agriculture	Rural economic development loans liquidating account*	0
446	Agriculture	Facilities acquisition and enhancement fund*	0
447	Housing and Urban Development	Homeownership assistance fund*	0
448	Housing and Urban Development	Consolidated fee fund*	0
449	Department of State	International Center, Washington, D.C.*	0
450	Interior	Donations and contributed funds*	0
451	Treasury	Collection Contractor Support*	0
452	Veterans Affairs	United States Government life insurance fund	0
453	Veterans Affairs	Medical facilities revolving fund*	0
454	Veterans Affairs	Veterans extended care revolving fund*	0
455	International Assistance Programs	Kuwait civil reconstruction trust fund*	0
456	Judicial Branch	United States Court of Federal Claims Judges' retirement fund	0
457	Legislative Branch	Compensation of members, Senate	0
458	Legislative Branch	Tax Court judges survivors annuity fund*	0
459	Agriculture	Emergency boll weevil loan program account*	0
460	Agriculture	Gifts and bequests	0
461	Agriculture	Apple loans program account*	0
462	Agriculture	Rural community fire protection grants*	0
463	Agriculture	National sheep industry improvement center revolving fund*	0
464	Agriculture	Land acquisition reinvestment fund*	0
465	Energy	Continuing fund, Southwestern Power Administration*	0
466	Energy	Advances for cooperative work*	0
467	Housing and Urban Development	Interstate land sales*	0
468	Department of State	Foreign service national defined contributions retirement fund*	0
469	Department of State	USIA Foreign Service national separation liability trust fund*	0
470	Interior	Dutch John community assistance*	0

Table 19. (Continued)

Dollars in millions			
Obs. #	**Agency**	**Account**	**5-year avg. dollar change (absolute value)**
471	Transportation	Saint Lawrence Seaway Development Corporation*	0
472	Transportation	Minority business resource center program*	0
473	Federal Financial Institutions Examination Council Appraisal Subcommittee	Registry fees	0
474	International Assistance Programs	Private sector revolving fund liquidating account*	0
475	Japan-United States Friendship Commission	Japan-United States Friendship trust fund	0
476	National Credit Union Administration	Community development credit union revolving loan fund*	0
477	Other Defense Civil Programs	Wildlife conservation	0
478	Other Defense Civil Programs	Soldiers' and airmen's home revolving fund*	0
479	Other Defense Civil Programs	White House commission on the national moment of remembrance*	0
480	Allowances	Contingent offset for the refundable portion of the health care tax credit*	0
481	Barry Goldwater Scholarship and Excellence in Education Foundation	Barry Goldwater Scholarship and Excellence in Education Foundation	0
482	Agriculture	P.L. 480 title I food for progress credits, program account*	0
483	Commerce	Gifts and bequests	0
484	Department of Defense—Military	Concurrent receipt accrual payments to the Military Retirement Fund*	0
485	Department of Defense—Military	Restoration of the Rocky Mountain Arsenal*	0
486	Education	Reading excellence*	0
487	Education	School construction*	0
488	Education	Class size reduction and teacher financing*	0
489	Education	Perkins loan revolving fund*	0
490	Educationa	Federal family education loan insurance fund*	0
491	Health and Human Services	State legalization impact assistance grants*	0
492	Health and Human Services	Health maintenance organization loan and loan guarantee fund*	0

Table 19. (Continued)

Dollars in millions			
Obs. #	Agency	Account	5-year avg. dollar change (absolute value)
493	Homeland Security	Disaster assistance direct loan program account*	0
494	Housing and Urban Development	Empowerment zones/enterprise communities*	0
495	Justice	Civil liberties public education fund*	0
496	Labor	Foreign labor certification processing*	0
497	Interior	Bureau of Reclamation loan program account*	0
498	Interior	Miscellaneous permanent appropriations*	0
499	Interior	Payment to tribe, Lower Brule Sioux Trust Fund*	0
500	Interior	Miscellaneous Indian trust payments*	0
501	Interior	Operation and maintenance of quarters*	0
502	Interior	Operation and maintenance of quarters*	0
503	Interior	Fee collection support, national park system*	0
504	Interior	National park renewal fund*	0
505	Interior	Concessions improvement accounts*	0
506	Interior	Park concessions franchise fees*	0
507	Interior	African elephant conservation fund*	0
508	Interior	Miscellaneous permanent appropriations*	0
509	Treasury	Payment to Justice, FIRREA related claims*	0
510	Treasury	Payments to the farm credit system financial assistance corporation liquidating account*	0
511	Treasury	Miscellaneous activities to be authorized in tobacco legislation*	0
512	Treasury	Miscellaneous permanent appropriations*	0
513	Transportation	Railroad rehabilitation and improvement program*	0
514	Transportation	Aviation user fees	0
515	Veterans Affairs	Veterans housing benefit program fund*	0
516	Veterans Affairs	Reinstated entitlement program for survivors under P.L. 97-377*	0
517	Veterans Affairs	Miscellaneous veterans housing loans guaranteed loan financing account*	0
518	Veterans Affairs	Medical care cost recovery fund*	0
519	District of Columbia	District of Columbia Federal pension fund*	0
520	District of Columbia	Federal payment for water and sewer services*	0
521	Environmental Protection Agency	Revolving fund for certification and other services*	0
522	General Services Administration	Working capital fund*	0

Table 19. (Continued)

Dollars in millions			
Obs. #	Agency	Account	5-year avg. dollar change (absolute value)
523	General Services Administration	Acquisition workforce training fund*	0
524	General Services Administration	Pennsylvania Avenue activities*	0
525	General Services Administration	Land acquisition and development fund*	0
526	International Assistance Programs	Payment to the Foreign Service retirement and disability fund	0
527	Judicial Branch	Payment to judiciary trust funds	0
528	Legislative Branch	Gifts and donations*	0
529	Legislative Branch	United States Capitol Police memorial fund*	0
530	National Aeronautics and Space Administration	National Space Grant Program*	0
531	National Aeronautics and Space Administration	Science, space, and technology education trust fund	0
532	Other Independent Agencies	Foreign service national separation liability trust fund*	0
533	Other Independent Agencies	Miscellaneous trust funds*	0
534	Tennessee Valley Authority	Tennessee Valley Authority Office of the Inspector General*	0
	Total		**$162,987**

Source: GAO analysis of President's budget data.

Note: The shaded rows indicate the 7 case study accounts discussed in appendix I. Accounts with fewer than 5 years of data are denoted with an "*".

End Notes

[1] For more information, see GAO, *21st Century Challenges: Reexamining the Base of the Federal Government*, GAO-05-325SP (Washington, D.C.: February 2005).

[2] BEA established pay-as-you-go (PAYGO) rules to ensure that legislation affecting direct, or mandatory, spending and revenues was budget-neutral over each session of Congress. In addition, annual discretionary spending limits were established. The sequestration procedure enforced PAYGO rules and discretionary spending caps. See Pub. L. No. 101-508, title XIII, § 13204, 104 Stat. 1388, Nov. 5, 1990.

[3] GAO, *Budget Policy: Issues in Capping Mandatory Spending*, GAO/AIMD-94-155 (Washington, D.C.: July 18, 1994).

[4] GAO, *Fiscal Exposures: Improving the Budgetary Focus on Long-Term Costs and Uncertainties*, GAO-03-213 (Washington, D.C.: Jan. 24, 2003).

[5] GAO/AIMD-94-155.

[6] These seven accounts listed in the Objectives, Scope and Methodology section were selected because of the relatively large 5-year average differences between their estimated and actual outlays.

[7] Both the Congressional Budget Office (CBO) and the Office of Management and Budget (OMB) estimate the cost of bills that affect mandatory spending.

[8] BEA amended the Balanced Budget and Emergency Deficit Control Act of 1985, sometimes referred to as the Gramm-Rudman-Hollings Act. In this chapter, the amended Balanced Budget and Emergency Deficit Control Act of 1985 is referred to as the Budget Enforcement Act, or BEA.

[9] BEA defined mandatory spending (referred to as "direct spending" in BEA) as spending for entitlement authority, the Food Stamp program, and budget authority provided in laws other than appropriations acts. Mandatory programs include familiar benefits and services—among them Social Security, Food Stamps, and Medicare—as well as other lesser-known activities, such as revolving funds and certain activities of the National Park Service, the Bureau of Customs and Border Protection, and the federal judiciary.

[10] GAO/AIMD-94-155.

[11] Examples of these 2005 bills include S. 19, S. 568, H.R. 523, H.R. 903, and H.R. 2290.

[12] Given the size and breadth of programs covered by the Commodity Credit Corporation, we selected two programs within the large account: corn and crop disaster assistance.

[13] Although the source of Medicaid funding is through an annual appropriation act, Medicaid is not considered a discretionary spending program. Because Medicaid is an entitlement created by the operation of law, if Congress fails to appropriate money necessary to fund payments and benefits, eligible recipients may seek legal recourse. In such case, necessary payments may be made through the indefinite judgment fund pursuant to 31 U.S.C. § 1304.

[14] For more information on MMI, see GAO, *Mortgage Financing: FHA's $7 Billion Reestimate Reflects Higher Claims and Changing Loan Performance Estimates*, GAO-05-875 (Washington, D.C.: Sept. 2, 2005).

[15] In addition, these interest payments must be made in order to avoid a default on the federal government's debt obligations.

[16] GAO, *Budget Surpluses: Experiences of Other Nations and Implications for the United States*, GAO/AIMD-00-23 (Washington, D.C.: Nov. 2, 1999).

[17] As discussed earlier, BEA established pay-as-you-go (PAYGO) rules to ensure that legislation affecting direct spending and revenues was budget-neutral in each session of Congress. In addition, annual discretionary spending limits were established.

[18] For the purpose of the Medicare trigger, general revenue is defined as the difference between Medicare program outlays and dedicated Medicare financing sources. Dedicated Medicare financing sources are HI payroll taxes, the HI share of income taxes on Social Security benefits, state transfers for Part D prescription drug benefits, premiums paid under Parts A, B, and D, and any gifts received by the trust funds.

[19] Recently, this provision was included in the Bipartisan Retirement Security Act of 2005, H.R. 440, 109th Cong. § 14 (2005).

[20] CBO uses probabilistic modeling when the possible cost of a legislative proposal is not distributed symmetrically around a single, most likely outcome. For example, under marketing loan programs, low crop prices yield large costs to the government with farmers paying back loans at the lower market price rather than the higher loan rate. However, high crop prices provide no offsetting gains because farmers may simply repay their loans at the original loan rate. For more information, see CBO, *Estimating the Costs of One-Sided Bets: How CBO Analyzes Proposals with Asymmetric Uncertainties* (Washington, D.C.: Oct. 1999).

[21] Department of Defense and Emergency Supplemental Appropriations for Recovery from and Response to Terrorist Attacks on the United States, 2002, Pub. L. No. 107-117, Div. C, § 102, Jan. 10, 2002.

[22] CRS, *Fashioning a Tax Cut Trigger: Economic Issues*, Order Code RL30948 (Washington, D.C.: Updated Jan. 29, 2002).

[23] GAO-05-325SP.

[24] Although the SGR was designed to encourage fiscal discipline, administrative and legislative actions modified or overrode the SGR system, resulting in fee increases for 2003, 2004, and 2005. For more information on this, see GAO, *Medicare Physician Payments: Concerns about Spending Target System Prompt Interest in Considering Reform*, GAO-05-85 (Washington, D.C.: Oct. 8, 2004).

[25] States may keep Reed Distributions in their trust funds or appropriate the money for administrative costs. Because state funds are held by the U.S. Treasury, they are not recorded as an outlay until the states distribute the funds.

[26] GAO, *Long-Term Fiscal Issues: Increasing Transparency and Reexamining the Base of the Federal Budget*, GAO-05-317T (Washington, D.C.: Feb. 8, 2005).

[27] GAO, *Government Performance and Accountability: Tax Expenditures Represent a Substantial Federal Commitment and Need to Be Reexamined*, GAO-05-690 (Washington, D.C.: Sept. 23, 2005).

[28] Summing tax expenditure estimates does not take into account interactions between individual provisions.

[29] For additional details, see GAO, *Tax Policy: Tax Expenditures Deserve More Scrutiny*, GAO/GGD/AIMD-94-122 (Washington, D.C.: June 3, 1994).

[30] Given this chapter's focus on constraining growth in mandatory spending, our analysis focused more on underestimates than overestimates of actual outlays.

[31] If a new law has effects that differ from those reflected in CBO's initial estimate, the differences will appear as technical "reestimates" in later revisions to the baseline.

[32] In all cases, CBO had prepared scoring estimates of the legislation.

[33] Although Crop Disaster Assistance programs are generally funded through supplemental appropriations acts, the Department of Agriculture considers and applies funding in a manner similar to mandatory programs. According to a Farm Service Agency official, funding is provided to all eligible applications for assistance by prorating available funding if necessary. OMB also considers Crop Disaster Assistance programs to be mandatory in that all eligible applicants may receive benefits.

[34] The HI Trust Fund finances Medicare Part A while the SMI Trust Fund finances Medicare Part B.

[35] Federal commodity subsidies essentially consist of three types of payments available to supplement farmers' income: direct payments to historical producers of the commodity, countercyclical payments, which provide a safety net in the event of low crop prices, and nonrecourse loans, which allow farmers to store production and use loan proceeds to meet cash flow needs without selling the crop.

[36] Direct loan subsidy cost is the estimated long-term cost to the government of a direct loan excluding administrative costs. It is the net present value of estimated loan disbursements, repayments of principal, payments of interest, and other payments by or to the government over the life of the loan.

[37] The market basket refers to an input price index that reflects the cost of a particular type of health care provider (e.g., hospital, skilled nursing facility, home health agency) to provide services to patients. This index is used to update the payments to providers from one year to the next.

[38] Section 101(a) of BBRA provided for a temporary, 20 percent increase in per diem adjusted payment rates for 15 specified resource utilization groups. Under section 101(c) of the Act, this increase was to be effective for SNF services furnished on or after April 1, 2000, and would continue until the later of: (1) October 1, 2000, or (2) implementation of a refined case-mix classification system that would better account for medically-complex patients.

[39] The Commodity Credit Corporation budget account encompasses many programs that are influenced by different factors. Accordingly, to gain an appreciation for the factors that should be considered in designing budget triggers, we focused on two programs—corn and crop disaster assistance. These two programs experienced the greatest average 5-year differences between estimated and actual outlays.

[40] Given the nature of soft triggers, that is, requiring special consideration or reporting, to avoid redundancy we do not present soft triggered actions for each of the case study accounts.

[41] Farm Security Act and Rural Investment Act of 2002, Pub. L. No. 107-171 (May 13, 2002).

[42] According to USDA's Economic Research Service, the average change in annual U.S. farm sector production expenses between 2001 and 2005 was about 2.5 percent.

[43] For example, see Military Construction Appropriation and Emergency Hurricane Supplemental Appropriations Act, 2005, Pub. L. No. 108-324, 118 Stat. 1220, 1232-37, Oct. 13, 2005.

[44] GAO, *Budgeting for Emergencies: State Practices and Federal Implications*, GAO/AIMD-99-250 (Washington, D.C.: Sept. 30, 1999).

[45] Under the Federal Family Education Loan Program (FFELP), private lenders fund the loans and the government guarantees them a minimum yield and repayment if borrowers default. FFELP is a larger program than is FDLP in terms of both annual and outstanding loan volume.

[46] Loans made in each fiscal year are called a cohort.

[47] While using guaranteed loan data is appropriate for the interim, guaranteed loans may perform differently than FDLP loans. Accordingly, Education plans to phase out the use of guaranteed loan data as FDLP data become available.

[48] Higher Education Act of 1965 (Public Law 89-329), as amended, Section 455 (a)(1).

[49] Hereafter, all will be referred to as states.

[50] Pub. L. No. 108-27, §401, 117 Stat. 752, 764 (May 28, 2003).

[51] The premium for Part A was $375 per month in 2005. Medicare premiums can change each year.

[52] The portion of the HI trust fund that is not needed to cover current expenditures for administration and benefits is invested on a daily basis in interest-bearing obligations of the federal government.

[53] Public Law 108-173. In this chapter, the Medicare Prescription Drug, Improvement, and Modernization Act of 2003 is referred to as the Medicare Modernization Act (MMA).

[54] For the purpose of the Medicare trigger, general revenue is defined as the difference between Medicare program outlays and dedicated Medicare financing sources. Dedicated Medicare financing sources are HI payroll taxes, the HI share of income taxes on Social Security benefits, state transfers for Part D prescription drug benefits, premiums paid under Parts A, B, and D, and any gifts received by the trust funds.

[55] Physician spending was about 40 percent of total Part B benefits in fiscal year 2004.

[56] GAO, *Medicare Physician Payments: Considerations for Reforming the Sustainable Growth Rate System*, GAO-05-326T (Washington, D.C.: Feb. 10, 2005) and *Medicare Physician Payments: Concerns about Spending Target System Prompt Interest in Considering Reforms*, GAO-05-85 (Washington, D.C.: Oct. 8, 2004).

[57] Part B premiums have seen double-digit increases in the past 3 years, and are expected to continue in the future if Congress again decides to override the SGR.

[58] Reed Distributions occur when excess funds build up in federal accounts. States can keep the money in their trust funds or appropriate the money for administrative costs. Because these state funds are held by the U.S. Treasury, they are not recorded as an outlay until the states distribute the funds.

[59] Special Reed Distributions occur when Congress mandates a distribution to state UTF accounts but do not follow all the Reed Act provisions. Appendix II Analysis of Total Outlays, Receipts, and Fiscal Position

[60] Differences between estimated and actual discretionary outlays were much greater than for mandatory outlays. However, on the whole, differences in receipts outweighed differences in outlays.

[61] Budget figures discussed here are in constant 2004 dollars.

[62] A comparable figure showing total estimated and actual mandatory outlays for fiscal years 2000 through 2004 is included as figure 9.

In: Federal Spending: A Riddle Wrapped ... ISBN: 978-1-60741-728-6
Editor: Frederick C. Hargis

Chapter 5

TRENDS IN DISCRETIONARY SPENDING

Andrew Austin and Mindy R. Levit

ABSTRACT

Discretionary spending is provided in, and controlled by, annual appropriations acts, which fund many of the routine activities commonly associated with such federal government functions as running executive branch agencies, congressional offices and agencies, and international operations of the government. Essentially all spending on federal wages and salaries is discretionary. Discretionary spending is often contrasted with mandatory, or direct, spending. Mandatory spending includes federal spending on entitlement programs, the Food Stamp program, and other spending controlled by laws other than appropriation acts. Spending levels for mandatory programs are generally controlled by eligibility criteria and size of the eligible population.

SUMMARY

Discretionary spending is provided and controlled through appropriations acts, which fund many of the activities commonly associated with such federal government functions as running executive branch agencies, congressional offices and agencies, and international operations of the government. Essentially all spending on federal wages and salaries is discretionary.

FY2008 federal spending accounted for just over a fifth (20.9%) of the U.S. economy, nearly equal to its average share of gross domestic product (GDP) since FY1962. While discretionary spending was the largest component of federal spending until the mid-1970s, mandatory spending now accounts for about 3% more of GDP than discretionary spending.

From FY1962, when discretionary spending accounted for 47.2% of total outlays, to FY2008, discretionary spending's share of federal outlays has fallen by almost a fifth. Over time, discretionary spending has fallen as a percentage of GDP because it has grown slower than the overall economy. Rapid growth of entitlement outlays and slower growth in defense spending relative to other federal spending are two major causes of the long-term fall in discretionary spending's share of federal spending.

Discretionary spending is often divided into defense, domestic discretionary, and international outlays. Defense and domestic discretionary spending compose nearly all of discretionary spending. In FY1962, discretionary spending equaled 12.3% of GDP, with defense spending making up 9.0% of GDP. In FY2008, total discretionary spending fell to 7.9% of GDP with defense spending totaling 4.3% of GDP. However, over the last six years, military spending has increased sharply. On average, from FY1999 to FY2008, defense outlays grew 8% per year in real terms, while non-defense discretionary outlays grew 2.5% per year in real terms.

Increases in discretionary spending are likely over the next several fiscal years due to the current economic turmoil and resulting federal intervention to stimulate the economy. Over the long term, projected future growth in entitlement program outlays may put severe pressure on discretionary spending unless policies changes are enacted or federal revenues are increased.

WHAT DOES DISCRETIONARY SPENDING INCLUDE?[1]

Discretionary spending is provided in, and controlled by, annual appropriations acts, which fund many of the routine activities commonly associated with such federal government functions as running executive branch agencies, congressional offices and agencies, and international operations of the government.[2] Essentially all spending on federal wages and salaries is discretionary.[3]

Discretionary spending is often contrasted with mandatory, or direct, spending. Mandatory spending includes federal spending on entitlement programs, the Food Stamp program, and other spending controlled by laws other than appropriation acts.[4] Spending levels for mandatory programs are generally controlled by eligibility criteria and size of the eligible population.

Budget Authority and Outlays

The distinction between outlays and budget authority is important to understanding the federal budget and, particularly, discretionary spending. Appropriations legislation, which controls discretionary spending, grants budget authority to accomplish specific ends. Budget authority is what federal agencies can legally spend. Budget authority has been compared to funds deposited into a checking account, which then can be used for specified federal purposes. Outlays are disbursed federal funds. Therefore, an outlay is not recorded until the federal government disburses appropriated funds to purchase goods and services.

Table 1. Categories of Federal Spending

	Budget Authority Provided by Law Other than Appropriation Acts	**Budget Authority Provided by Appropriation Acts**
Entitlement	Medicare Social Security	Appropriated Entitlements (e.g., veterans' compensation, Medicaid, TANF) Food Stamps (with caveats)
Not an Entitlement	Salaries for Members of Congress Mandatory non-entitlements (e.g., Forest Service payments to states)	Discretionary Spending[a] (defense, non-defense domestic discretionary, and international)

Source: Compiled by CRS.

a. Discretionary spending programs. See discussion in text.

Table 1 illustrates the different categories of federal spending (i.e., mandatory and discretionary spending) by contrasting the type of budget authority needed for specific purposes.

Outlay data are used to assess the macroeconomic effects of the federal budgets, while budget analysis of specific federal programs is typically based on budget authority, because that is what Congress controls most directly.

Congressional appropriations, which grant budget authority for specific purposes, are not always tightly linked to changes in outlays in the following year. While budget authority can be granted for a single year, some appropriations (such as for many military construction projects) provide budget authority for multiple years, or indefinitely. Thus outlays that flow from an appropriated sum might be spread over several fiscal years, implying that budget authority totals will differ from outlay totals for a single fiscal year.[5]

TRENDS IN DISCRETIONARY SPENDING

The composition of the federal budget has changed dramatically since the early 1960s. Over time, the share of total discretionary spending in federal spending has fallen, while the share of mandatory spending has increased. Discretionary spending accounted for 67.5% of total outlays in FY1962, but only an estimated 38.1% of total outlays in FY2008.[6] Mandatory spending, by contrast, rose from 26.1% of total outlays in FY1962 to 53.7% in FY2008.

In contrast to the longer term trends, between FY1999 and FY2008, discretionary spending grew more quickly than mandatory spending. After falling for three decades between the late 1960s and the late 1990s, discretionary spending increased 5.1% a year in real terms on average from FY1999 to FY2008. Over the same period, the share of discretionary spending as a proportion of federal outlays grew from 33.6% in FY1999 to 38.1% in FY2008.

How has the Composition of Discretionary Spending Changed?

In FY1962, discretionary spending comprised 67.5% of total outlays, with mandatory spending and net interest accounting for 26.1% and 6.5%, respectively. Discretionary spending as a share of total outlays reached its peak in FY1963. By FY2008, discretionary spending fell to an estimated 38.1% of total outlays. Mandatory spending accounted for an estimated 53.7% of total outlays, with net interest at 8.2%in FY2008. **Figure 1** shows discretionary spending, mandatory spending, and net interest payments in relation to total outlays since 1962.

Another way to look at the changing composition of discretionary spending is to examine it as a share of GDP. Measuring budget components as a share of GDP compares their size to the economy as a whole. **Figure 2** shows components of federal spending as a percentage of GDP since FY1962. While discretionary spending was the largest component of federal spending until the mid 1970s, mandatory spending now accounts for about 3% more of GDP than discretionary spending. Medicare and Medicaid have continued to grow faster than overall federal spending, contributing to the majority of the increase in mandatory spending over this period. Social Security spending, the other large component of mandatory spending, has been relatively stable in the last decade when measured as a share of GDP.

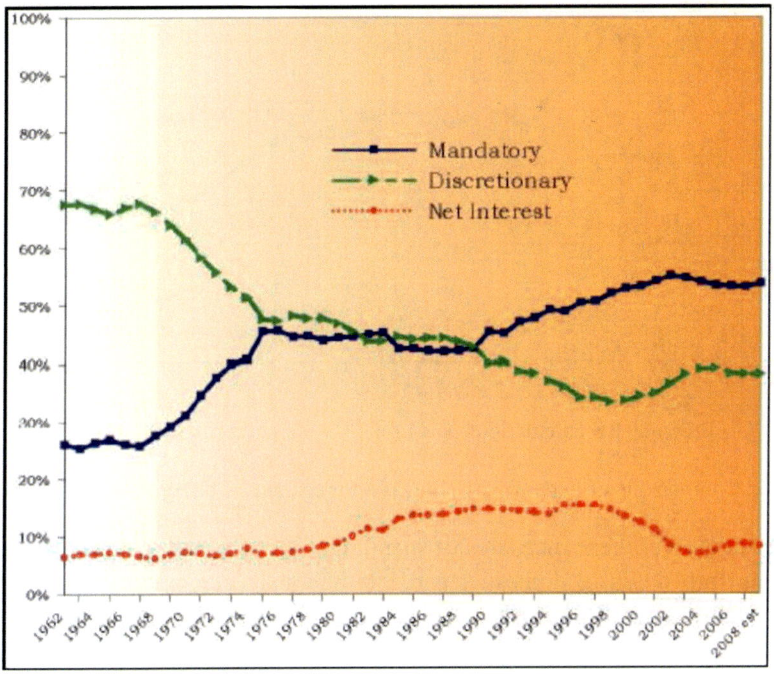

Source: OMB data, CRS calculations. Data for FY2008 are estimated.

Figure 1. Components of Federal Spending as a Percentage of Total Outlays, FY1962 – FY2008

Because of the decline in discretionary spending as a percentage of total outlays and the resulting increase in the share of mandatory spending over time, controlling the federal budget may have become more difficult for Congress. In other words, because mandatory spending is set automatically, less money is available to allocate to other government agencies and programs unless revenues rise or Congress modifies eligibility requirements and benefits of mandatory spending programs.

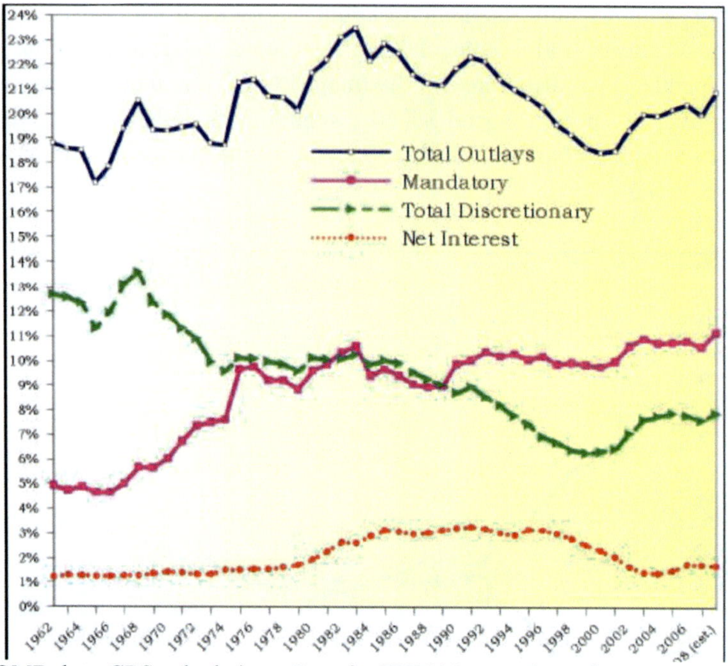

Source: OMB data, CRS calculations. Data for FY2008 are estimated.

Figure 2. Components of Federal Spending as a Percentage of GDP, FY1962-FY2008

In addition to these measures of spending, CBO also subdivides discretionary spending into defense, domestic, and international categories. **Figure 3** shows these categories of discretionary spending as a share of GDP over the period FY1962-FY2008. Defense spending, 73% of total discretionary spending in FY1962, accounted for 53.8% of discretionary spending in FY2008. In terms of GDP, discretionary defense spending fell from 9.5% GDP in FY1968 to 4.3% in FY2008. Over the same period, domestic and international discretionary spending have changed less dramatically as a percentage of GDP. Domestic discretionary spending did increase in the 1970s but has since fallen, remaining closer to its period average.

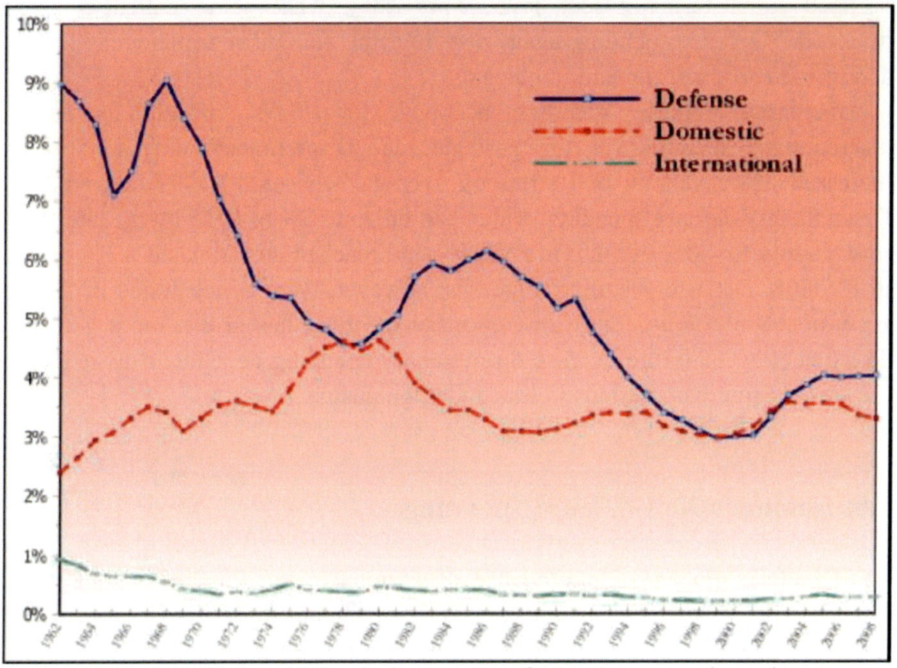

Source: CBO and OMB data, CRS calculations. Data for FY2008 are estimated.

Figure 3. Discretionary Outlays by Type, FY1962-FY2008

Discretionary Defense Spending

Since the late 1960s, defense spending grew more slowly than federal spending in other areas. Some contend that defense expenditures as a proportion of GDP should be expected to fall over the long term because the cost of defending the nation depends on factors that are largely independent of economic growth.

Defense spending increased sharply in the mid-1960s as the United States' involvement in Vietnam deepened. After large-scale withdrawals of American troops from Vietnam began in 1969, defense spending as a share of GDP fell for the next decade. The Soviet invasion of Afghanistan prompted the Carter Administration, and then the Reagan Administration, to boost military expenditures resulting in an increase in defense spending during the early 1980s. After the Berlin Wall was opened in November 1989 and communist governments in central and eastern Europe collapsed, defense spending as a share of GDP dropped to historically low levels, providing what some called a "peace dividend." Defense spending again rose after the attacks of September 11, 2001, and wars in Afghanistan and Iraq began.

Increased defense spending accounts for 75.6% of the increase in discretionary spending in the past decade. Discretionary defense spending increased 8% a year in real terms on average between FY1999 and FY2008.[7] Discretionary defense spending, which had fallen to 3% of GDP by the late 1990s, rose sharply to 4.0% of GDP in FY2005, and reached an estimated 4.3% of GDP in FY2008. Defense spending increases, however, were concentrated in the past six years, while non-defense discretionary spending has grown more gradually. The trajectory of future defense discretionary spending depends in large part on the scale of future operations in Iraq and Afghanistan.

Discretionary Non-defense Spending

Trends in domestic non-defense discretionary spending are less dramatic. Non-defense spending supports the largest number of federal agencies and programs, including foreign affairs, science and technology research, natural resources, energy, education, and numerous others. None of the individual programs within the non-defense discretionary category have approached 1% of GDP since FY1962. Most of these programs spent less than 0.5% of GDP during that period.

Domestic non-defense discretionary spending, 2.5% of GDP in 1962, rose to a peak of 4.8% in 1980. Domestic non-defense discretionary spending's share of GDP fell during the Reagan Administration, reaching 3.1% of GDP in FY1987.[8] Since then it has fluctuated between 3.0% and 3.7% of GDP. CBO estimates that FY2008 domestic non-defense discretionary spending will account for 3.7% of GDP.

Discretionary International Spending

Discretionary spending for international programs since FY1962 has averaged 0.4% of GDP, reaching its peak of 1.0% of GDP in FY1962. Since that time, international spending has generally trended downward. Between FY2001 and FY2008, spending on international programs rose from 0.2% of GDP to 0.3% of

GDP. The majority of the funding in this category in recent times has been devoted to diplomatic missions, foreign aid, and international finance.

Although discretionary spending has increased rapidly in the past half decade, spending in some government departments and agencies has grown very slowly or has been cut, while spending in other areas has expanded rapidly. Funding for defense and emergency and disaster management increased sharply in the wake of hurricane Katrina, boosting overall discretionary spending further. In recent years, disaster funding has dropped sharply, allowing non-defense spending as a share of GDP to fall as well.

THE FY2009 BUDGET AND BEYOND

Congress and the President will begin dealing with budget issues in early 2009. Due to the transition to the Obama Administration, however, budget details might be unavailable in early February, thus effectively compressing the Congressional budget cycle and shortening the time available for Congress to review budget proposals. New shocks to the financial system and the economy may present Congress with new demands for federal responses. Federal spending tied to means-tested social programs has been increasing due to rising unemployment, while federal revenues will likely fall as individuals' incomes drop and corporate profits sink. Funding requests for military operations in Iraq and Afghanistan will likely continue. New policies and requests, if implemented, could affect discretionary spending levels in FY2009.

In his final budget submission, President Bush's FY2009 budget called for limiting growth in defense and non-defense discretionary spending during the five years FY2009-FY2013. The proposals would reduce total discretionary spending in dollars, in real terms, as a share of GDP, and as a percentage of total federal spending over the five-year period. The 110th Congress enacted few of these proposed cuts in discretionary spending.

In President Bush's budget proposal, discretionary defense spending would rise from $549.2 billion in FY2007 to $670.7 billion in FY2009. After FY2009, proposed defense outlays fall, although this is largely due to the omission of war costs. Continuing current levels of war funding over the coming five years would slow the fall in defense spending as a percentage of GDP. The Bush Administration projected a fall in discretionary defense spending to 3.1% of GDP in FY2013.[9] The Bush Administration has made a priority of holding down growth in "non-security" discretionary spending.[10] After rising slightly in FY2008 and FY2009 from $493 billion in FY2007, the Bush Administration proposed decreases in non-defense spending by FY2013.

CURRENT SITUATION

Most non-defense discretionary spending programs are now operating under a continuing resolution through March 6, 2009. With the inauguration of the new President, budgetary priorities may change as the new Administration and Congress confront ongoing financial and economic challenges while facing the need to complete funding for the remainder of FY2009 and begin consideration of the FY2010 budget. Given the current state of the economy, significant increases in discretionary spending, at least over the next several years, are likely.

The federal government has responded to this financial turmoil with an extraordinary set of measures. In February 2008, Congress enacted a $152 billion package (P.L. 110-185, Economic Stimulus Act of 2008) to stimulate consumption that sent refunds to taxpayers and let firms depreciate their capital more quickly. Later in the year, the Federal Reserve created a panoply of lending facilities to provide financial institutions with loans in exchange for various types of collateral. On October 3, Congress passed the Emergency Economic Stabilization Act of 2008 (EESA; P.L. 110-343), which authorized the Treasury Secretary to use $700 billion (subject to certain Congressional restrictions and notifications) to intervene in financial markets or to inject capital into key financial institutions as part of a Troubled Assets Relief Program (TARP).

In response to economic downturn, federal spending has increased and revenues have decreased. Slow growth is expected for the next few years. As the beginning of the 111th Congress approaches, many economists believe that another large fiscal stimulus is in order. The size, variety, and complexity of new stimulus in addition to previous federal responses to this turmoil present many challenges to budget analysis. The ultimate costs of these responses and their budgetary impact, especially with regard to discretionary spending levels, will depend on how the economy performs, how well firms with federal credit guarantees weather future financial shocks, and whether the government receives positive returns on its asset purchases.

DISCRETIONARY SPENDING IN THE LONG TERM

The annual budget process, and the appropriations decisions in particular, provide Congress with the ability to change, continue, or reverse trends in discretionary spending. If discretionary spending were held constant in real terms, as the CBO baseline presumes, then discretionary spending per capita would decrease as population grows and it would shrink as a share of GDP as the economy grows. On average the U.S. population grew 1% a year and per capita GDP grew 2.25% per year from 1962 to 2005.[11] If those trends were to persist, then holding discretionary spending constant in real terms implies per capita discretionary spending would shrink by 1% a year and discretionary spending as a share of the economy would shrink by 3.25% per year.

Due to the current economic downturn, large-scale fiscal stimulus and aggressive spending measures intended to mitigate systematic risks in financial markets may be needed to limit serious damage to the economy. When economic recovery begins, and as soon as appropriate, many economists and policy makers hope that spending increases used to stimulate the economy will be reversed. At that point, it is suggested that attention turn to deficit reduction.

Over the long run, growth in entitlement spending will present severe fiscal challenges. Recent research on long-term fiscal challenges has focused on continued increases in the per beneficiary cost of health care, as well as the more predictable demographic changes that will occur as the baby boom generation retires. Projections from a variety of sources predict that spending on Medicare and Social Security will increase sharply as a share of GDP in coming decades.[12] CBO projects that Medicare will expand from 5.6% of GDP in 2030 to 14.8% in 2082 and that Social Security will grow from 6.1% of GDP in 2030 to 6.4% of GDP by 2082. Federal Medicaid outlays, 1.4% of GDP in FY2007, are projected to reach 17.6% of GDP in 2050.[13]

Social Security, Medicare, and Medicaid outlays as a proportion of GDP are projected to equal or exceed the present share of federal revenues as a proportion of GDP (17.7% in FY2007) sometime after the middle of the 21st century. Maintaining current levels of discretionary spending would then require either substantial tax increases or major changes in those entitlement programs.

End Notes

[1] This chapter was originally written by Philip Winters, who has retired from CRS.

[2] Annual appropriations acts fall within the jurisdiction of the House and Senate Appropriations Committees.

[3] Exceptions exist. For example, salaries for Members of Congress, the President, and federal judges are classified as mandatory spending, as are essentially all federal retirement and disability costs. Direct spending is controlled by committees with legislative jurisdiction.

[4] For more information, see CRS Report RL33074, *Mandatory Spending Since 1962*, by D. Andrew Austin and Mindy R. Levit.

[5] While federal officials often have some discretion to choose how quickly appropriated funds are spent, they face constraints imposed by legislation designed to protect Congress's power of the purse. According to the Anti-Deficiency Act, a federal official cannot spend government money beyond what is available through appropriations or a fund by law. See General Accountability Office, *Antideficiency Act Background*, available at http://www.gao.gov/ada/antideficiency.htm for code citations and explanations. The Congressional Budget Act and Impoundment Control Act of 1974 (P.L. 93-344) limits the ability of federal officials to withhold or delay spending of appropriated funds without Congressional approval.

[6] CBO figures for discretionary and mandatory spending and their components are used in all calculations. The Bureau of Economic Analysis GDP deflator is used to adjust for inflation.

[7] FY2008 data are estimated. Defense discretionary spending includes enacted supplemental requests.

[8] For a summary of Reagan-era spending changes, see David Stockman, *The Triumph of Politics* (New York: Harper&Row, 1986), pp. 401-411.

[9] General Mike Mullen, Chairman of the Joint Chiefs of Staff, noted in an interview that the defense budget was now "just under 4% of GDP," and stated that "... I would see that in the future as an absolute floor." *New York Times*, October 22, 2007. Transcript available at http://www.nytimes.com/2007/10/22/washington/22mullen-text.html.

[10] The Bush Administration defined "security" discretionary funding as spending on the Department of Defense, Government-wide Homeland Security activities, and International Affairs.

[11] These figures based on CRS calculations derived from CBO and Census Bureau data.

[12] See CBO, "*The Long-Term Budget Outlook*," December 2007; point 10 of the United States of America—2006 Article IV Consultation, Concluding Statement of the IMF Mission, May 31, 2006; and CRS Report RL33623, *Long- Term Measures of Fiscal Imbalance*, by D. Andrew Austin.

[13] CBO, "The Long-Term Budget Outlook: An Update," December 2007.

CHAPTER SOURCES

The following chapters have been previously published:

Chapter 1 – This is an edited, excerpted and augmented edition of a United States Congressional Research Service publication, Report Order Code RS22354, dated January 8, 2009.

Chapter 2 –These remarks were delivered as Statement of David M. Walker, Comptroller General of the United States, before the Budget Committee, House of Representatives, in a United States Government Accountability Office (GAO), Publication GAO-06-456T, dated February 15, 2006.

Chapter 3 – This is an edited, excerpted and augmented edition of a United States Congressional Research Service publication, Report Order Code RL33074, dated December 17, 2008.

Chapter 4 - This is an edited, excerpted and augmented edition of a United States Government Accountability Office (GAO), Report to Congressional Committees. Publication GAO-06-276, dated January 2006.

Chapter 5 – This is an edited, excerpted and augmented edition of a United States Congressional Research Service publication, Report Order Code RL34424, dated December 23, 2008.

INDEX

C

D

E

F

G

H

I

J

L

M

N

O

P

Q

R

S

T

U

V

W

Y